New Perspectives on
Microsoft®
Windows® 95

BRIEF

The New Perspectives Series

The New Perspectives Series consists of texts and technology that teach computer concepts and the programs listed below. Both Windows 3.1 and Windows 95 versions of these programs are available. You can order these New Perspectives texts in many different lengths, software releases, bound combinations, and CourseKits ™. Contact your CTI sales representative or customer service representative for the most up-to-date details.

The New Perspectives Series

Computer Concepts

dBASE

Internet and the World Wide Web

Lotus 1-2-3

Microsoft Access

Microsoft Excel

Microsoft Office Professional

Microsoft PowerPoint

Microsoft Windows 3.1

Microsoft Windows 95

Microsoft Word

Microsoft Works

Novell Perfect Office

Paradox

Presentations

Quattro Pro

WordPerfect

New Perspectives on

Microsoft®
Windows® 95

June Jamrich Parsons
University of the Virgin Islands

Dan Oja
GuildWare, Inc.

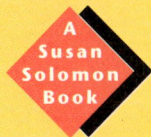

A Susan Solomon Book

COURSE TECHNOLOGY, INC.

A DIVISION OF COURSE TECHNOLOGY

COMMUNICATIONS GROUP

ONE MAIN STREET, CAMBRIDGE MA 02142

AN INTERNATIONAL THOMSON PUBLISHING COMPANY

I(T)P

Albany • Bonn • Boston • Cincinnati • London • Madrid • Melbourne • Mexico City
New York • Paris • San Francisco • Singapore • Tokyo • Toronto • Washington

New Perspectives on Microsoft Windows 95 — Brief is published by Course Technology, Inc.

Managing Editor	Mac Mendelsohn
Series Consulting Editor	Susan Solomon
Product Manager	Susan Solomon
Production Editor	Catherine D. Griffin
Text and Cover Designer	Ella Hanna
Cover Illustrator	Nancy Nash

© 1996 by Course Technology, Inc.
A Division of International Thomson Publishing, Inc.

For more information contact:

Course Technology, Inc.
One Main Street
Cambridge, MA 02142

International Thomson Editores
Campos Eliseos 385, Piso 7
Col. Polanco
11560 Mexico D.F. Mexico

International Thomson Publishing Europe
Berkshire House 168-173
High Holborn
London WCIV 7AA
England

International Thomson Publishing GmbH
Kônigswinterer Strasse 418
53227 Bonn
Germany

Thomas Nelson Australia
102 Dodds Street
South Melbourne, 3205
Victoria, Australia

International Thomson Publishing Asia
211 Henderson Road
#05-10 Henderson Building
Singapore 0315

Nelson Canada
1120 Birchmount Road
Scarborough, Ontario
Canada M1K 5G4

International Thomson Publishing Japan
Hirakawacho Kyowa Building, 3F
2-2-1 Hirakawacho
Chiyoda-ku, Tokyo 102
Japan

Trademarks
Course Technology and the open book logo are registered trademarks of Course Technology, Inc.
I(T)P The ITP logo is a trademark under license.
Microsoft and Windows 95 are registered trademarks of Microsoft Corporation.

Some of the product names and company names used in this book have been used for identification purposes only and may be trademarks or registered trademarks of their respective manufacturers and sellers.

Disclaimer
Course Technology, Inc. reserves the right to revise this publication and make changes from time to time in its content without notice.

ISBN 1-56527-287-0

Printed in the United States of America

10 9 8 7 6 5 4 3

From the New Perspectives Team

At Course Technology, Inc., we have one foot in education and the other in technology. We believe that technology is transforming the way people teach and learn, and we are excited about providing instructors and students with materials that use technology to teach about technology.

Our development process is unparalleled in the higher education publishing industry. Every product we create goes through an exacting process of design, development, review, and testing.

Reviewers give us direction and insight that shape our manuscripts and bring them up to the latest standards. Every manuscript is quality tested. Students whose backgrounds match the intended audience work through every keystroke, carefully checking for clarity and pointing out errors in logic and sequence. Together with our own technical reviewers, these testers help us ensure that everything that carries our name is error-free and easy to use.

We show both *how* and *why* technology is critical to solving problems in college and in whatever field you choose to teach or pursue. Our time-tested, step-by-step instructions provide unparalleled clarity. Examples and applications are chosen and crafted to motivate students.

As the New Perspectives Series team at Course Technology, our goal is to produce the most timely, accurate, creative, and technologically sound product in the entire college publishing industry. We strive for consistent high quality. This takes a lot of communication, coordination, and hard work. But we love what we do. We are determined to be the best. Write us and let us know what you think. You can also e-mail us at info@course.com.

The New Perspectives Series Team

Joseph Adamski	Kathy Finnegan	Karla Mitchell
Judy Adamski	Robin Geller	Dan Oja
Roy Ageloff	Chris Greacen	June Parsons
David Auer	Roger Hayen	Sandra Poindexter
Rachel Bunin	Charles Hommel	Ann Shaffer
Joan Carey	Chris Kelly	Susan Solomon
Patrick Carey	Terry Ann Kremer	John Zeanchock
Barbara Clemens	Melissa Lima	Beverly Zimmerman
Kim Crowley	Mac Mendelsohn	Scott Zimmerman
Jessica Evans		

Preface ^{The New Perspectives Series}

What is the New Perspectives Series?

Course Technology, Inc.'s **New Perspectives Series** combines text and technology products that teach computer concepts and microcomputer applications. Users consistently praise this series for innovative pedagogy, creativity, supportive and engaging style, accuracy, and use of interactive technology. The first New Perspectives text was published in January of 1993. Since then, the series has grown to more than thirty titles and has become the best-selling series on computer concepts and microcomputer applications. Others have imitated the New Perspectives features, design, and technologies, but none have replicated its quality and its ability to consistently anticipate and meet the needs of instructors and students.

How is the New Perspectives Series different from other microcomputer applications series?

The **New Perspectives Series** distinguishes itself from other series in at least four substantial ways: sound instructional design, consistent quality, innovative technology, and proven pedagogy. The texts in this series consist of two or more tutorials, which are based on sound instructional design. Each tutorial is motivated by a realistic case that is meaningful to students. Rather than learn a laundry list of features, students learn the features in the context of solving a problem. This process motivates all concepts and skills by demonstrating to students why they would want to know them.

Instructors and students have come to rely on the high quality of the **New Perspectives Series** and to consistently praise its accuracy. This accuracy is a result of Course Technology's unique multi-step quality assurance process that incorporates student testing at three stages of development, using hardware and software configurations appropriate to the product. All solutions, test questions, and other Course Tools (see below) are tested using similar procedures. Instructors who adopt this series report that students can work through the tutorials independently, with a minimum of intervention or "damage control" by instructors or staff. This consistent quality has meant that if instructors are pleased with one product from the series, they can rely on the same quality with any other New Perspectives product.

The **New Perspectives Series** also distinguishes itself by its innovative technology. This series innovated truly *interactive* learning applications—CTIWinApps, Interactive Labs, and CTI Windows 95 Applications. These applications have set the standard for interactive learning.

How do I know that the New Perspectives Series will work?

Some instructors who use this series report a significant difference between how much their students learn and retain with this series as compared to other series. With other series, instructors often find that students can work through the book and do well on homework and tests, but still not demonstrate competency when asked to perform particular tasks outside the context of the text's sample case or project. With the **New Perspectives Series**, however, instructors report that students have a complete, integrative learning experience that stays with them. They credit this high retention and competency to the fact that this series incorporates critical thinking and problem solving with computer skills mastery.

How does this book I'm holding fit into the New Perspectives Series?

New Perspectives microcomputer applications books are available in seven categories—**Brief, Introductory, Intermediate, Comprehensive, Advanced, Four-in-One,** and **Five-in-One.**

Brief books are about 100 pages long and are intended to teach only the essentials of the particular microcomputer application. The book you are holding is a Brief book.

Introductory books are about 300 pages long and consist of 6 or 7 tutorials. An Introductory book is designed for a short course on a particular application or for a one-term course to be used in combination with other Introductory books.

Four-in-One books and **Five-in-One** books combine a Brief book on Windows with 3 or 4 Introductory books. For example, *New Perspectives on Microsoft Office* is a Five-in-One book—it combines Brief Windows with Introductory Word, Excel, Access, and PowerPoint.

Comprehensive books consist of all of the tutorials in the Introductory book, plus 3 or 4 more tutorials on more advanced topics. They also include Brief Windows tutorials, an *Essential Computer Concepts* chapter, 3 or 4 Additional Cases, and a Reference Section.

Intermediate books take the 3 or 4 tutorials at the end of three Comprehensive books and combine them. Reference Sections and Additional Cases are also included.

Advanced books begin by covering topics similar to those in the Comprehensive books, but cover them in more depth. Advanced books then go on to present the most high-level coverage in the series.

Finally, as the name suggests, **Concepts and Applications** books combine the *New Perspectives on Computer Concepts* book with various Brief and Introductory microcomputer applications books.

New Perspectives Series Applications Titles

Legend: ■ Brief   ■ Introductory   ■ Essential Computer Concepts   ■ Comprehensive   ■ Advanced

Brief	Introductory	Four-In-One	Five-In-One	Comprehensive	Intermediate	Advanced
2 to 4 Tutorials	Brief + 4 or 5 more Tutorials	Essential Computer Concepts + Brief Windows + 3 Introductory	Essential Computer Concepts + Brief Windows + 4 Introductory	Brief Windows + 1 Introductory + 3 or 4 Comprehensive Tutorials + Additional Cases + Reference Sections	3 or 4 Tutorials from 4 books + Additional Cases + Reference Sections	Quick review of basics + in-depth, high-level coverage

In what kind of course could I use this book?

This book can be used in any course in which you want students to learn just the basics of Windows 95—the essentials of Windows 95 navigation and file management. This book assumes that students have had no prior computer experience.

How do the Windows 95 editions differ from the Windows 3.1 editions?

Larger Page Size If you've used a *New Perspectives* text before, you'll immediately notice that the book you're holding is larger than the Windows 3.1 series books. We've responded to user requests for a larger page, which allows for larger screen shots and associated callouts. Look on page 24 for an example of how we've made the screen shots easier to read.

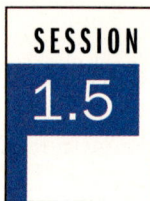

SESSION 1.5

Sessions We've divided the tutorials into sessions. Each session is designed to be completed in about 45 minutes to an hour (depending, of course, upon student needs and the speed of your lab equipment). With sessions, learning is broken up into more easily-assimilated chunks. You can more accurately allocate time in your syllabus. Students can more easily manage the available lab time. Each session begins with a "session box," which quickly describes which skills the student will learn in the session. Furthermore, each session is numbered, which makes it easier for you and your students to navigate and communicate about the tutorial. Look on page 14 for the session box that opens Session 1.2.

Quick Check

Quick Checks Each session concludes with meaningful, conceptual questions—called Quick Checks—that test students' understanding of what they learned in the session. The answers to all of the Quick Check questions are at the back of the book preceding the Index. You can find examples of Quick Checks on pages 13, 25, and 40.

New Design We have retained a design that helps students easily differentiate between what they are to *do* and what they are to *read*. The steps are easily identified by their shaded background and numbered steps. Furthermore, this new design presents steps and screen shots in a larger, easier to read format. Some good examples of our new design are pages 22 and 23, and 30 and 31.

What features are retained in the Windows 95 editions of the New Perspectives Series?

"Read This Before You Begin" Page This page is consistent with Course Technology's unequaled commitment to helping instructors introduce technology into the classroom. Technical considerations and assumptions about hardware and software are listed in one place to help instructors save time and eliminate unnecessary aggravation. The "Read This Before You Begin" page for this book is on page 2.

CASE

Tutorial Case Each tutorial begins with a problem presented in a case that is meaningful to students. The problem turns the task of learning how to use an application into a problem-solving process. The problems increase in complexity with each tutorial. These cases touch on multicultural, international, and ethical issues—so important to today's business curriculum. In this book the Tutorial Case is about a student working in a Windows 95 lab for the first time. The case begins on page 3.

Windows 95 Brief **Task Reference**

TASK	PAGE #	RECOMMENDED METHOD	NOTES
Character, delete	33	Press Backspace	
Check box, de-select	21	Click the check box again	Tab to option, press Spacebar
Check box, select	21	Click the checkbox	Tab to option, press Spacebar
Detailed file list, view	45	From My Computer, click View, Details	
Disk, copy your	50	Place disk in drive A:, from My Computer click [3½ Floppy (A:)], click File, Copy Disk, Start	See "Making a Backup of Your Floppy Disk."
Disk, format	30	Click [My Computer], click [3½ Floppy (A:)], press Enter, click File click Format, click Start	
Drop-down list, display	20	Click [▼]	
File, copy		From My Computer, right-click the file, drag to the new location, press C	
File, delete	49	From My Computer, click the file, press Delete, click Yes	See "Deleting a File."
File, move	48	From My Computer, use the left mouse button to drag the file to the desired folder or drive	See "Moving a File."
File, open	37	Click [icon]	
File, print	39	Click [icon]	
File, print preview	39	Click [icon]	
File, rename	49	From My Computer, click the file, click File, click Rename, type new name, press Enter	See "Renaming a File."
File, save	35	Click [icon]	
Folder, create	46	From My Computer, click File, New, Folder	See "Creating a New Folder."
Help topic, display	23	From the Help Contents window, click the topic, then click Open	
Help topic, open	23	From the Help Contents window, click the book, then click Display	
Help, start	21	Click [Start], then click Help	F1, See "Starting Windows 95 Help."
Icon, open	43	Click the icon, then press Enter or double-click the icon	See "Opening an Icon."

Windows 95 Brief **Task Reference**

TASK	PAGE #	RECOMMENDED METHOD	NOTES
Icons, view large	45	From My Computer, click View, Large Icons	
Insertion point, move	34	Click the desired location in the document Use arrow keys	
List box, scroll	20	Click ▲ or ▼, or drag the scroll box	
Menu option, select	17	Click the menu option	
Menu, open		Click the menu option	Alt-underlined letter
Program, quit	10	Click ✕	Alt-F4
Program, start	9	Click the Start button, point to Programs, point to the program option, click the program	See "Starting a Program."
Radio button, de-select	21	Click a different radio button	Tab to option, press Spacebar
Radio button, select	21	Click the radio button	Tab to option, press Spacebar
Start menu, display			Ctrl-Esc
Student data disk, create	41	Click ▣ Start, click Programs, CTI Win95, Windows 95 Brief, Make Windows 95 Student Disk, press Enter	
Text, select	34	Drag the pointer over the text	
Tooltip, display	19	Position pointer over the tool	
Window, change size	17	Drag ◩	
Window, close	10	Click ✕	Ctrl-F4
Window, maximize	17	Click ▢	
Window, minimize	15	Click ▬	
Window, move	17	Drag the title bar	
Window, redisplay	16	Click the taskbar button	
Window, restore	16	Click ▣	
Window, switch	12	Click the taskbar button of the program	Alt-Tab, See "Switching Between Programs."
Windows 95, shut down	12	Click ▣ Start, click Shut Down, Click Yes	
Windows 95, start	5	Turn on the computer	

1.
2.
3.

Step-by-Step Methodology   This unique Course Technology methodology keeps students on track. They click or press keys always within the context of solving the problem posed in the tutorial case. The text constantly guides students, letting them know where they are in the course of solving the problem. In addition, the numerous screen shots include labels that direct students' attention to what they should look at on the screen. On almost every page in this book, you can find an example of how steps, screen shots, and callouts work together.

TROUBLE?

TROUBLE? *Paragraphs*   TROUBLE? paragraphs anticipate the mistakes that students are likely to make and help them recover from these mistakes. By putting these paragraphs in the book, rather than in the instructor's manual, we facilitate independent learning and free the instructor to focus on substantive conceptual issues rather than on common procedural errors. Two representative examples of Troubles? are on pages 32 and 33.

3.1 NOTE

3.1 Notes   Many students who use this book might have already used Windows 3.1 in preceding classes or on the job. The 3.1 Notes are designed to answer likely questions, head off likely confusions, and point out helpful bits of information for students who have some previous experience with Windows 3.1. Look on pagess 10 and 37 for examples of 3.1 Notes.

REFERENCE window

Reference Windows   Reference Windows appear throughout the text. They are short, succinct summaries of the most important tasks covered in the tutorials. Reference Windows are specially designed and written so students can refer to them for their reference value when doing the Tutorial Assignments and Case Problems, and after completing the course. Page 12 contains the Reference Window for Switching Between Programs.

Task Reference   The Task Reference is a summary of how to perform commonly-used tasks using the most efficient method, as well as helpful shortcuts. It appears as a table at the end of the book. In this book the Task Reference is on pages 63–64.

Tutorial Assignments, Case Problems, and Lab Assignments   Each tutorial concludes with Tutorial Assignments, which provide students with additional hands-on practice of the skills they learned in the tutorial. The Tutorial Assignments are followed by four Case Problems that have approximately the same scope as the tutorial case. In the Windows 95 applications texts, there is always one Case Problem in the book and one in the Instructor's Manual that do not use a presupplied student file, requiring students to solve the problem from scratch. Finally, if a Lab (see below) accompanies the tutorial, Lab Assignments are included. Look on pages 52 through 54 for the Tutorial Assignments for Tutorial 2. This Brief book does not contain Case Problems. Examples of Lab Assignments are on page 28.

E XPLORE

Exploration Exercises   The Windows environment allows students to learn by exploring and discovering what they can do. Exploration Exercises can be Tutorial Assignments or Case Problems that might challenge students, encourage them to explore the capabilities of the program they are using, and extend their knowledge using the Windows Help facility and other reference materials. Page 27 contains Exploration Exercises for Tutorial 1.

The New Perspectives Series is known for using technology to help instructors teach and administer, and to help students learn. What Course Tools are available with this textbook?

All of the teaching and learning materials available with the **New Perspectives Series** are known as Course Tools.

Course Labs   Computer skills and concepts come to life with the New Perspectives Course Labs—highly interactive tutorials that guide students step-by-step, present them with Quick Check questions, allow them to explore on their own, and test them on their comprehension. Lab Assignments are also included in the book at the end of each relevant tutorial. The labs available with this book and the tutorials in which they appear are:

Using a Keyboard -
Tutorial 1

Using a Mouse -
Tutorial 1

Using Files -
Tutorial 2

Course Test Manager   Course Test Manager is cutting edge Windows-based testing software that helps instructors design and administer pre-tests, practice tests, and actual examinations. The full-featured program provides random test generation of practice tests, immediate on-line feedback, and generation of detailed study guides for questions that are incorrectly answered. On-line pre-tests help instructors assess student skills and plan instruction. Also, students can take tests at the computer; tests can be automatically graded and generate statistical information for the instructor on individual and group performance. Instructors can also use Course Test Manager to produce printed tests.

Course Presenter   Course Presenter is a CD ROM-based presentation tool that provides instructors with a wealth of resources for use in the classroom, replacing traditional overhead transparencies with computer-generated screenshows. Presenter gives instructors the flexibility to create custom presentations, complete with matching student notes and lecture notes pages. The presentations integrate closely with the New Perspectives book and other Course Tools, and provide instructors with another resource to use so they can teach the way they want to teach.

Online Companions   When you use a New Perspectives product you are able to access Course Technology's Online Companion. Instructors may use the Faculty Online Companion for additional instructors' materials. Please see your Instructor's Manual or call your Course Technology customer service representative for more information. Students may access their Online Companion in the Student Center on the World Wide Web at http://www.vmedia.com/cti/.

Instructor's Manual Instructor's Manuals are written by the author(s) and are quality-assurance tested. Each Instructor's Manual includes some or all of the following items:

- Answers and solutions to all of the Quick Checks, Tutorial Assignments, Case Problems, and Additional Cases. Suggested solutions are also included for the Exploration Exercises. This is available in both hardcopy and digital form.
- A Setup Disk, which contains the software that installs the CTI Windows 95 Applications menu choices and all of the data files that students will use for the Tutorials, the Tutorial Assignments, and the Case Problems. A README file includes other technical tips for lab management.
- Troubleshooting Tips, which anticipate commonly-encountered problems.
- Transparency Masters of key concepts.
- Extra Problems and Additional Cases, to augment teaching options.
- Instructor's Notes, prepared by the authors and based on their teaching experience.

Acknowledgments

We want to thank all of the New Perspectives Team members for giving us input on essential Windows 95 skills. Their insights and team spirit were invaluable. Thanks also to the unequaled QA testing and technology support from Jeff Goding and Jim Valente; the pull-out-all-the-stops production work of Kim Munsell, Ella Hanna, Cathie Griffin, Patty Stephan, Kathryn Dinovo, and all the staff at Gex; and the demand-the-best-quality editorial support of Susan Solomon and Mac Mendelsohn. No thanks to Marilyn.

June Jamrich Parsons
Dan Oja

Brief Contents

Table of **Contents**

TUTORIAL 1
Exploring the Basics
Your First Day in the Lab   3

TUTORIAL 2
Working with Files
Your First Day in the Lab—Continued   29

New Perspectives on

Microsoft®
Windows® 95

BRIEF

TUTORIALS

Read This **Before You Begin**

STUDENT DISKS

To complete the tutorials and Tutorial Assignments, you need a Student Disk. Your instructor will either provide you with a Student Disk or ask you to make your own.

If you are supposed to make your own Student Disk, you will need a blank, formatted high-density disk. Follow the instructions in the section called "Creating Your Student Disk" in Tutorial 2 to use the Make Student Disk program to create your own Student Disk. See the inside front or inside back cover of this book for more information on Student Disk files, or ask your instructor or technical support person for assistance.

COURSE LABS

This book features three interactive Course Labs to help you understand Windows concepts. There are Lab Assignments at the end of each tutorial that relate to these Labs. To start a Lab, click the Start button on the Windows 95 taskbar, point to Programs, point to CTI Windows 95 Applications, point to Windows 95 New Perspectives Brief, and click the name of the Lab you want to use.

USING YOUR OWN COMPUTER

If you are going to work through this book using your own computer, you need:

■ **Computer System** Windows 95 must be installed on your computer. This book assumes a complete installation of Windows 95.

■ **Student Disk** Ask your instructor or lab manager for details on how to get the Student Disk. You will not be able to complete the tutorials or exercises in this book using your own computer until you have the Student Disk. The student files may also be obtained electronically over the Internet. See the inside front or inside back cover of this book for more details.

■ **Course Labs** See your instructor or technical support person to obtain the Course Lab software for use on your own computer.

To complete the tutorials and Tutorial Assignments in this book, your students must use a set of files on a Student Disk. The Instructor's Resource Kit for this book includes either two Student Files Setup Disks or a CD-ROM containing the student disk setup program. Follow the instructions on the disk label or in the Readme file to install the Make Student Disk program onto your server or standalone computers. Your students can then use the Windows 95 Start menu to run the program that will create their Student Disk. Tutorial 2 contains steps that instruct your students on how to generate student disks.

If you prefer to provide Student Disks rather than letting students generate them, you can run the Make Student Disk program yourself following the instructions in Tutorial 2.

COURSE LAB SOFTWARE

This book features three online, interactive Course Labs that introduce basic Windows concepts. The Instructor's Resource Kit for this book contains the Lab software either on four Course Labs Setup Disks or on a CD-ROM. Follow the instructions on the disk label or in the Readme file to install the Lab software on your server or standalone computers. Refer also to the Readme file for essential technical notes related to running the labs in a multiuser environment.
Once you have installed the Course Lab software, your students can start the Labs from the Windows 95 desktop by clicking the Start button on the Windows 95 taskbar, pointing to Programs, pointing to CTI Windows 95 Applications, pointing to Windows 95 New Perspectives Brief, and then clicking the name of the Lab they want to use.

CT LAB SOFTWARE AND STUDENT FILES

You are granted a license to copy the Student Files and Course Labs to any computer or computer network used by students who have purchased this book.

Exploring the Basics

Investigating the Windows 95 Operating System in the Computer Lab

Your First Day in the Lab

CASE

You walk into the computer lab and sit down at a desk. There's a computer in front of you, and you find yourself staring dubiously at the stack of software manuals. Where to start? As if in answer to your question, your friend Steve Laslow appears.

Gesturing to the stack of manuals, you tell Steve that you were just wondering where to start.

"You start with the operating system," says Steve. Noticing your slightly puzzled look, Steve explains that the **operating system** is software that helps the computer carry out basic operating tasks such as displaying information on the computer screen and saving data on your disks. Your computer uses the **Microsoft Windows 95** operating system—Windows 95, for short.

Steve tells you that Windows 95 has a "gooey" or **graphical user interface (GUI)**, which uses pictures of familiar objects, such as file folders and documents, to represent a desktop on your screen. Microsoft Windows 95 gets its name from the rectangular-shaped work areas, called "windows," that appear on your screen.

Steve continues to talk as he sorts through the stack of manuals on your desk. He says there are two things he really likes about Windows 95. First, lots of software is available for computers that have the Windows 95 operating system and all this software has a standard graphical user interface. That means once you have learned how to use one Windows software package, such as word-processing software, you are well on your way to understanding how to use other Windows software. Second, Windows 95 lets you use more than one software package at a time, so you can easily switch between your word-processing software and your appointment book software, for example. All in all, Windows 95 makes your computer an effective and easy-to-use productivity tool.

Steve recommends that you get started right away by using some tutorials that will teach you the skills essential for using Microsoft Windows 95. He hands you a book and assures you that everything on your computer system is set up and ready to go.

You mention that last summer you worked in an advertising agency where the employees used something called Windows 3.1. Steve explains that Windows 3.1 is an earlier version of the Windows operating system. Windows 95 and Windows 3.1 are similar, but Windows 95 is more powerful and easier to use. Steve says that as you work through the tutorials you will see notes that point out the important differences between Windows 95 and Windows 3.1.

Steve has a class, but he says he'll check back later to see how you are doing.

Using the Tutorials Effectively

These tutorials will help you learn about Windows 95. The tutorials are designed to be used at a computer. Each tutorial is divided into sessions. Watch for the session headings, such as Session 1.1 and Session 1.2. Each session is designed to be completed in about 45 minutes, but take as much time as you need. It's also a good idea to take a break between sessions.

Before you begin, read the following questions and answers. They are designed to help you use the tutorials effectively.

Where do I start?

Each tutorial begins with a case, which sets the scene for the tutorial and gives you background information to help you understand what you will be doing in the tutorial. Read the case before you go to the lab. In the lab, begin with the first session of the tutorial.

How do I know what to do on the computer?

Each session contains steps that you will perform on the computer to learn how to use Windows 95. Read the text that introduces each series of steps. The steps you need to do at a computer are numbered and are set against a color background. Read each step carefully and completely before you try it.

How do I know if I did the step correctly?

As you work, compare your computer screen with the corresponding figure in the tutorial. Don't worry if your screen display is somewhat different from the figure. The important parts of the screen display are labeled in each figure. Check to make sure these parts are on your screen.

What if I make a mistake?

Don't worry about making mistakes—they are part of the learning process. Paragraphs labeled **"TROUBLE?"** identify common problems and explain how to get back on track. Follow the steps in a **TROUBLE?** paragraph *only* if you are having the problem described. If you run into other problems:

- Carefully consider the current state of your system, the position of the pointer, and any messages on the screen.

- Complete the sentence, "Now I want to...." Be specific, because you are identifying your goal.

- Develop a plan for accomplishing your goal, and put your plan into action.

How do I use the Reference Windows?

Reference Windows summarize the procedures you learn in the tutorial steps. Do not complete the actions in the Reference Windows when you are working through the tutorial. Instead, refer to the Reference Windows while you are working on the assignments at the end of the tutorial.

How can I test my understanding of the material I learned in the tutorial?

At the end of each session, you can answer the Quick Check questions. The answers for the Quick Checks are at the end of the book.

After you have completed the entire tutorial, you should complete the Tutorial Assignments. The Tutorial Assignments are carefully structured so you will review what you have learned and then apply your knowledge to new situations.

What if I can't remember how to do something?

You should refer to the Task Reference at the end of the book; it summarizes how to accomplish commonly performed tasks.

What are the 3.1 Notes?

The 3.1 Notes are helpful if you have used Windows 3.1. The notes point out the key similarities and differences between Windows 3.1 and Windows 95.

What are the Interactive Labs, and how should I use them?

Interactive Labs help you review concepts and practice skills that you learn in the tutorial. Lab icons at the beginning of each tutorial and in the margins of the tutorials indicate topics that have corresponding Labs. The Lab Assignments section includes instructions for how to use each Lab.

Now that you understand how to use the tutorials effectively, you are ready to begin.

SESSION

1.1

In this session, in addition to learning basic Windows terminology, you will learn how to use a mouse, to start and stop a program, and to use more than one program at a time. With the skills you learn in this session, you will be able to use Windows 95 to start software programs.

Using a Keyboard

Starting Windows 95

Windows 95 automatically starts when you turn on the computer. Depending on the way your computer is set up, you might be asked to enter your user name and password. If prompted to do so, type your assigned user name and press the Enter key. Then type your password and press the Enter key to continue.

To start Windows 95:

1. Turn on your computer.

TROUBLE? If the Welcome to Windows 95 box appears on your screen, press the Enter key to close it.

The Windows 95 Desktop

In Windows terminology, the screen represents a **desktop**—a workspace for projects and the tools needed to manipulate those projects. Look at your screen display and locate the objects labeled in Figure 1-1 on the following page.

Because it is easy to customize the Windows environment, your screen might not look exactly the same as Figure 1-1. You should, however, be able to locate objects on your screen similar to those in Figure 1-1.

Icons are small pictures that represent objects such as your computer, your computer network, a specific computer program, or a document. Your desktop probably contains several icons, such as My Computer, Network Neighborhood, and the Recycle Bin. You'll use these icons in later tutorials to work with files stored on your computer or on other computers on the network.

Figure 1-1 ◀
The Windows
95 desktop

The **desktop** is
your workspace
on the screen.

The **Start** button
is one of the
most important
controls in
Windows 95.
You use the
Start button
to access essential
Windows 95
functions, programs,
and documents.

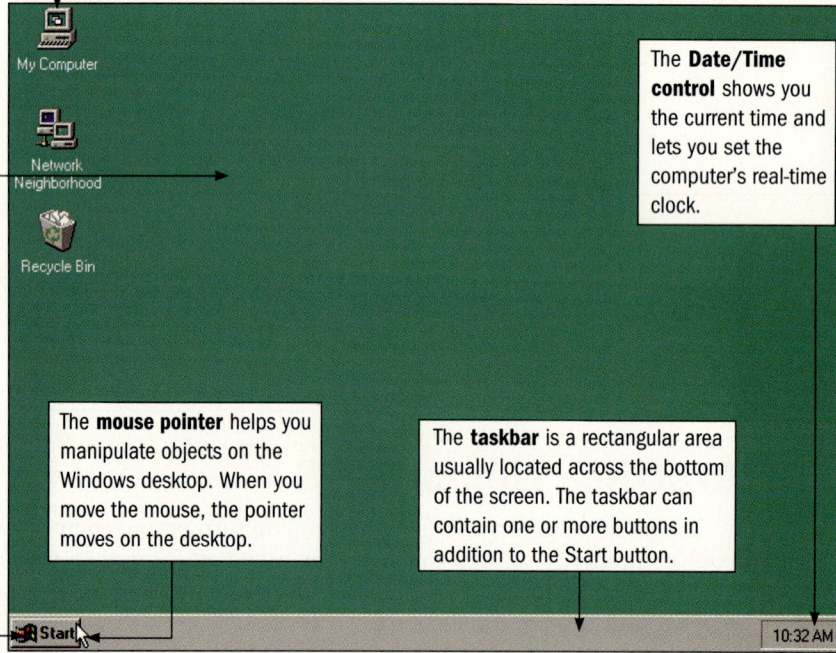

The **Date/Time control** shows you the current time and lets you set the computer's real-time clock.

My Computer

Network Neighborhood

Recycle Bin

The **mouse pointer** helps you manipulate objects on the Windows desktop. When you move the mouse, the pointer moves on the desktop.

The **taskbar** is a rectangular area usually located across the bottom of the screen. The taskbar can contain one or more buttons in addition to the Start button.

Start   10:32 AM

TROUBLE? If the screen goes blank or starts to display a moving design, press any key to restore the image.

Using the Mouse

Using a Mouse

A **mouse**, like those shown in Figure 1-2, is a pointing device that helps you interact with objects on the screen. In Windows 95 you need to know how to use the mouse to point, click, and drag. In this session you will learn about pointing and clicking. In Session 1.2 you will learn how to use the mouse to drag objects.

You can also interact with objects by using the keyboard; however, the mouse is much more convenient for most tasks, so the tutorials in this book assume you are using one.

Pointing

The **pointer**, or **mouse pointer**, is a small object that moves on the screen when you move the mouse. The pointer is usually shaped like an arrow. As you move the mouse on a flat surface, the pointer on the screen moves in the direction corresponding to the movement of the mouse. The pointer sometimes changes shape depending on where it is on the screen or the action the computer is completing.

Find the arrow-shaped pointer on your screen. If you do not see the pointer, move your mouse until the pointer comes into view.

Figure 1-2 ◀
The mouse

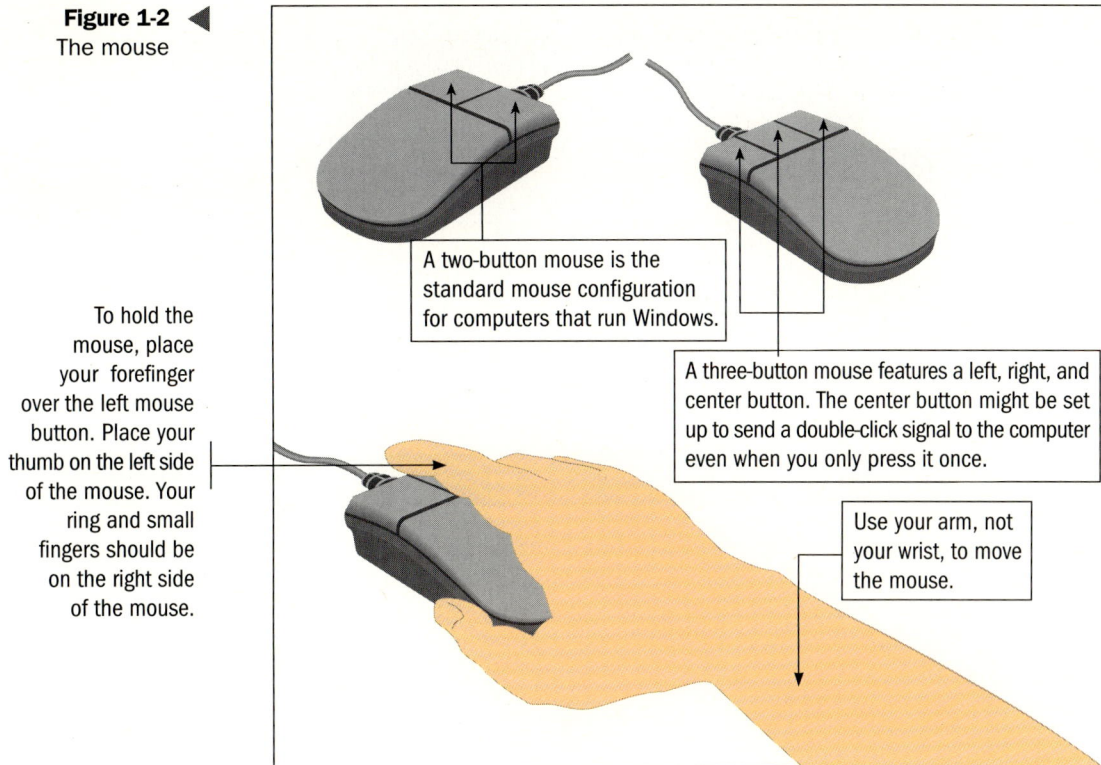

To hold the mouse, place your forefinger over the left mouse button. Place your thumb on the left side of the mouse. Your ring and small fingers should be on the right side of the mouse.

A two-button mouse is the standard mouse configuration for computers that run Windows.

A three-button mouse features a left, right, and center button. The center button might be set up to send a double-click signal to the computer even when you only press it once.

Use your arm, not your wrist, to move the mouse.

Basic "mousing" skills depend on your ability to position the pointer. You begin most Windows operations by positioning the pointer over a specific part of the screen. This is called **pointing**.

To move the pointer:

1. Position your right index finger over the left mouse button, as shown in Figure 1-2. Lightly grasp the sides of the mouse with your thumb and little finger.

TROUBLE? If you want to use the mouse with your left hand, ask your instructor or technical support person to help you use the Control Panel to change the mouse settings to swap the left and right mouse buttons. Be sure you find out how to change back to the right-handed mouse setting, so you can reset the mouse each time you are finished in the lab.

2. Locate the arrow-shaped pointer on the screen.

3. Move the mouse and watch the movement of the pointer.

If you run out of room to move your mouse, lift the mouse and move it to a clear area on your desk, then place the mouse back on the desk. Notice that the pointer does not move when the mouse is not in contact with the desk.

When you position the mouse pointer over certain objects, such as the objects on the taskbar, a "tip" appears. These "tips" are called **ToolTips**, and they tell you the purpose or function of an object.

To view ToolTips:

1. Use the mouse to point to the **Start** button ▣Start . After a few seconds, you see the tip "Click here to begin" as shown in Figure 1-3 on the following page.

Figure 1-3 ◀
Viewing ToolTips

Start button ──────

pointer   tip

Click here to begin

Sta   10:33 AM

TROUBLE? If you accidentally pressed a mouse button, press it again to get the Start menu off your screen.

2. What tip appears when you point to the date on the right end of the taskbar?

Clicking

When you press a mouse button and immediately release it, it is called **clicking**. Clicking the mouse selects an object on the desktop. *You usually click the left mouse button, so* unless the instructions tell you otherwise, always click the left mouse button.

Windows 95 shows you which object is selected by highlighting it, usually by changing the object's color, putting a box around it, or making the object appear to be pushed in, as shown in Figure 1-4.

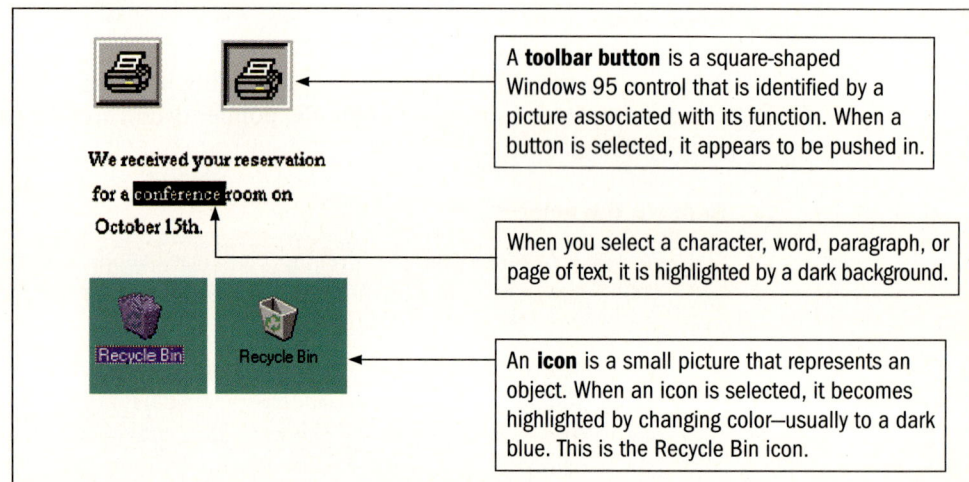

Figure 1-4 ◀
Selected objects

We received your reservation for a conference room on October 15th.

Recycle Bin   Recycle Bin

A **toolbar button** is a square-shaped Windows 95 control that is identified by a picture associated with its function. When a button is selected, it appears to be pushed in.

When you select a character, word, paragraph, or page of text, it is highlighted by a dark background.

An **icon** is a small picture that represents an object. When an icon is selected, it becomes highlighted by changing color—usually to a dark blue. This is the Recycle Bin icon.

To select the Recycle Bin icon:

1. Position the pointer over the **Recycle Bin** icon.

2. Click the mouse button and notice how the color of the icon changes to show that it is selected.

Starting and Closing a Program

The software you use is sometimes referred to as a program or an application. To use a program, such as a word-processing program, you must first start it. With Windows 95 you start a program by clicking the Start button. The Start button displays a menu.

A **menu** is a list of options. Windows 95 has a **Start menu** that provides you with access to programs, data, and configuration options. One of the Start menu's most important functions is to let you start a program.

The Reference Window below explains how to start a program. Don't do the steps in the Reference Window now; they are for your later reference.

REFERENCE window

STARTING A PROGRAM

- Click the Start button.
- Point to Programs.
- Point to the group that contains your program.
- Click the name of the program you want to run.

3.1 NOTE

WordPad is similar to Write in Windows 3.1.

Windows 95 includes an easy-to-use word-processing program called WordPad. Suppose you want to start the WordPad program and use it to write a letter or report.

To start the WordPad program from the Start menu:

1. Click the **Start** button 📖Start as shown in Figure 1-5. A menu appears.

Figure 1-5 ◀
Starting the
WordPad program

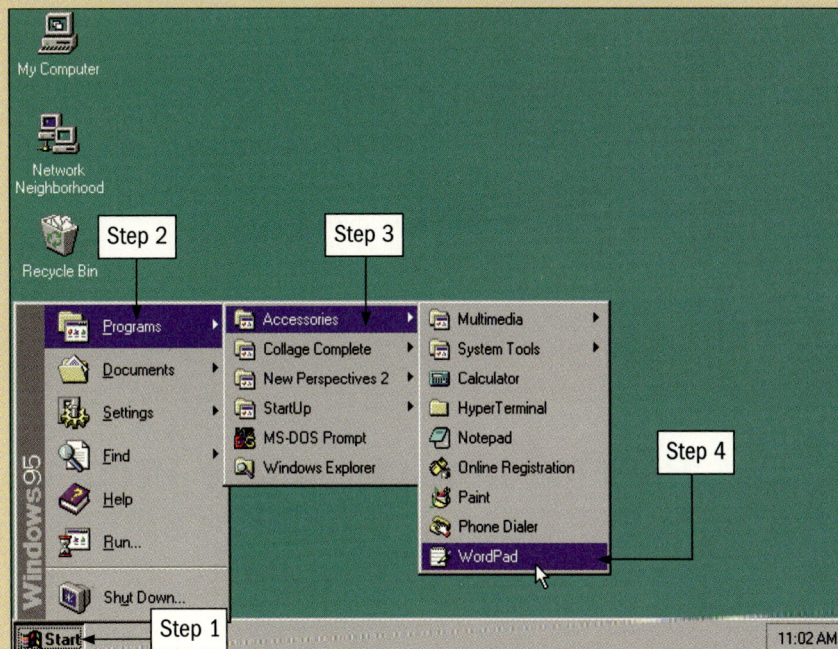

2. Point to **Programs**. After a short pause, the next menu appears.

    TROUBLE? If you don't get the correct menu, go back and point to the correct menu option.

3. Point to **Accessories**. Another menu appears.

4. Click **WordPad**. Make sure you can see the WordPad program as shown in Figure 1-6 on the following page.

Figure 1-6
The WordPad
program

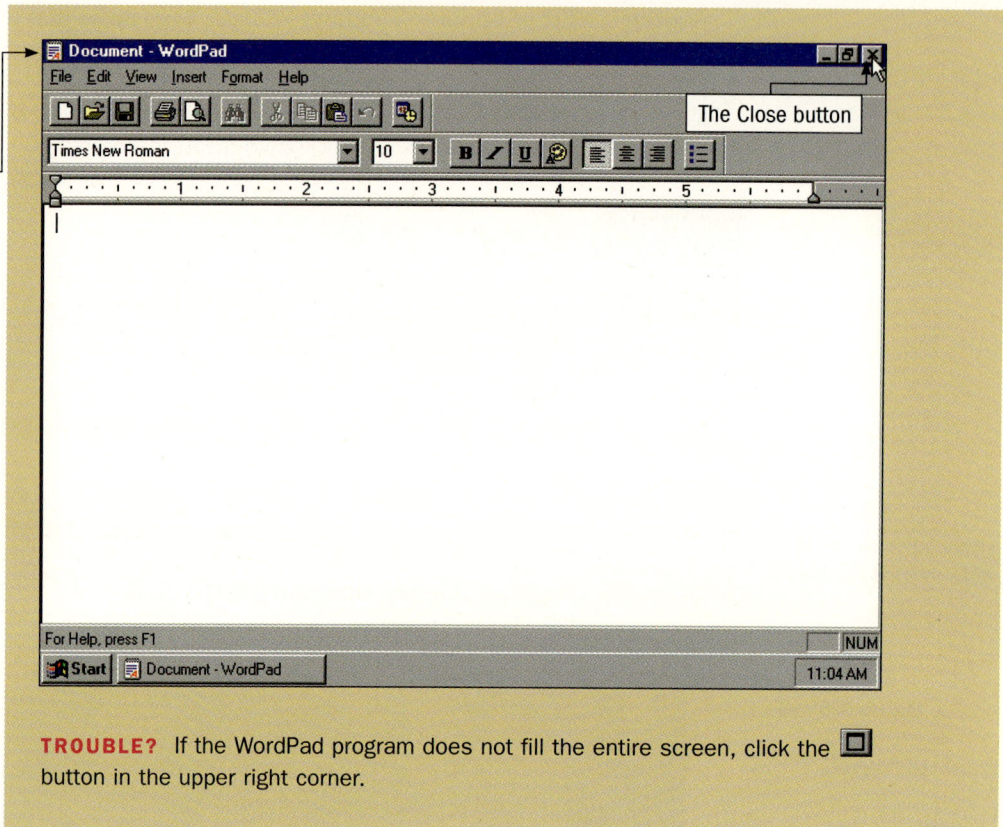

WordPad program
window

[Screenshot of WordPad program window titled "Document - WordPad" with menus File, Edit, View, Insert, Format, Help. Toolbar, "Times New Roman" font, size 10, formatting buttons. "The Close button" labeled at upper right. Ruler and blank document area. Status bar "For Help, press F1" and "NUM". Taskbar with Start button, "Document - WordPad", and "11:04 AM".]

TROUBLE? If the WordPad program does not fill the entire screen, click the ⬜ button in the upper right corner.

3.1 NOTE

As with Windows 3.1,
in Windows 95 you
can also exit a
program using the
Exit option from the
File menu.

When you are finished using a program, the easiest way to return to the Windows 95 desktop is to click the Close button ✖.

To exit the WordPad program:

1. Click the **Close** button ✖. See Figure 1-6. You will be returned to the Windows 95 desktop.

Running More than One Program at the Same Time

3.1 NOTE

Paint in Windows 95
is similar to
Paintbrush in
WIndows 3.1.

One of the most useful features of Windows 95 is its ability to run multiple programs at the same time. This feature, known as **multi-tasking**, allows you to work on more than one task at a time and to quickly switch between tasks. For example, you can start WordPad and leave it running while you then start the Paint program.

To run WordPad and Paint at the same time:

1. Start WordPad.

   TROUBLE? You learned how to start WordPad earlier in the tutorial: Click the Start button, point to Programs, point to Accessories, and then click WordPad.

2. Now you can start the Paint program. Click the **Start** button 🏁Start again.

3. Point to **Programs**.

4. Point to **Accessories**.

5. Click **Paint**. The Paint program appears as shown in Figure 1-7. Now two programs are running at the same time.

TROUBLE? If the Paint program does not fill the entire screen, click the ▢ button in the upper right corner.

Figure 1-7
The Paint
Program

Paint program
window

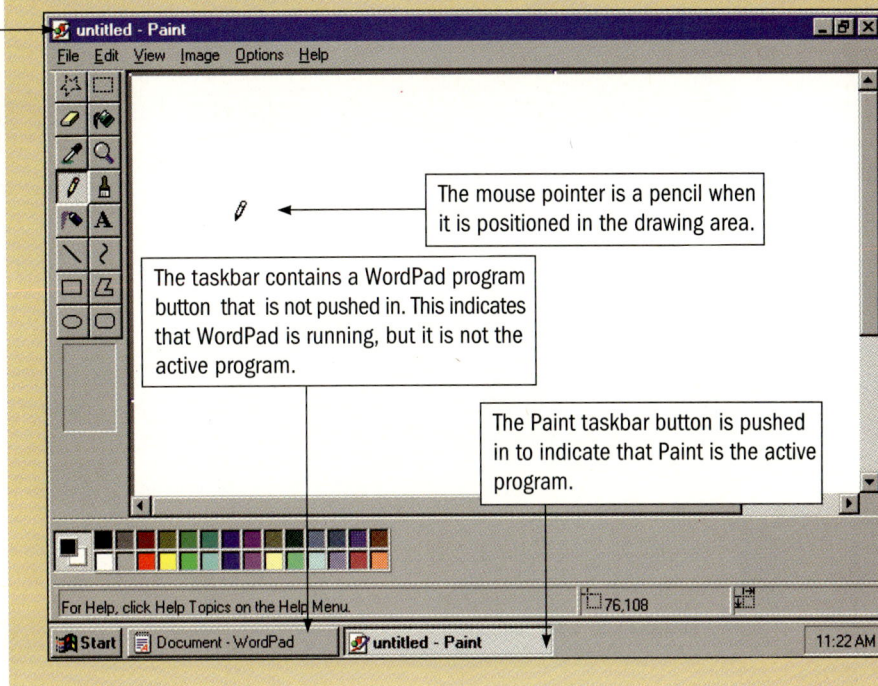

The mouse pointer is a pencil when it is positioned in the drawing area.

The taskbar contains a WordPad program button that is not pushed in. This indicates that WordPad is running, but it is not the active program.

The Paint taskbar button is pushed in to indicate that Paint is the active program.

For Help, click Help Topics on the Help Menu.   76,108

Start   Document - WordPad   untitled - Paint   11:22 AM

3.1 NOTE

With Windows 3.1, some users had difficulty finding program windows on the desktop. The buttons on the Windows 95 taskbar make it much easier to keep track of which programs are running.

What happened to WordPad? The WordPad button is still on the taskbar, so even if you can't see it, WordPad is still running. You can imagine that it is stacked behind the Paint program, as shown in Figure 1-8.

Other projects might be hidden under the project you are working on. For example, you might have worked on a letter earlier, but it is now under the picture you are currently drawing.

You might keep other projects handy on your desk. Anytime you want to work with one of them, you bring it to the center of your desk.

Figure 1-8
Programs
stacked on top
of a desk

Think of your screen as the main work area of your desk.

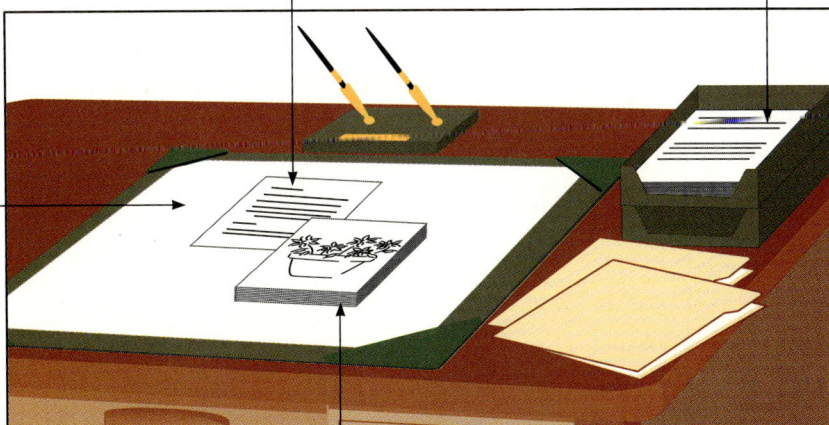

The project with which you are currently working is in your main work area. This project might be a multi-page document.

Switching Between Programs

3.1 NOTE

In Windows 95, you can still use Alt-Tab to switch between programs. You can also click any open window to switch to it.

Although Windows 95 allows you to run more than one program, only one program at a time is active. The **active** program is the program with which you are currently working. The easiest way to switch between programs is to use the buttons on the taskbar.

REFERENCE window

SWITCHING BETWEEN PROGRAMS

■ Click the taskbar button that contains the name of the program to which you want to switch.

To switch between WordPad and Paint:

1. Click the button labeled **Document - WordPad** on the taskbar. The Document - WordPad button now looks like it has been pushed in to indicate it is the active program.

2. Next, click the button labeled **untitled - Paint** on the taskbar to switch to the Paint program.

Closing WordPad and Paint

It is good practice to close each program when you are finished using it. Each program uses computer resources such as memory, so Windows 95 works more efficiently when only the programs you need are open.

To close WordPad and Paint:

1. Click the **Close** button ☒ for the Paint program. The button labeled "untitled - Paint" disappears from the taskbar.

2. Click the **Close** button ☒ for the WordPad program. The WordPad button disappears from the taskbar, and you return to the Windows 95 desktop.

Shutting Down Windows 95

It is very important to shut down Windows 95 before you turn off the computer. If you turn off your computer without correctly shutting down, you might lose data and damage your files.

To shut down Windows 95:

1. Click the **Start** button 🏁 Start on the taskbar to display the Start menu.

2. Click the **Shut Down** menu option to display the Shut Down Windows dialog box.

3. Make sure the **Shut down the computer?** option is selected.

4. Click the **Yes** button.

5. Wait until you see a message indicating it is safe to turn off your computer, then switch off your computer.

You should typically use the option "Shut down the computer?" when you want to turn off your computer. However, other shut-down options are available. For example, your school might prefer that you select the option to "Close all programs and log on as a different user." This option logs you out of Windows 95, leaves the computer turned on, and allows another user to log on without restarting the computer. Check with your instructor or technical support person for the preferred method for your school's computer lab.

Quick Check

1. Label the components of the Windows 95 desktop in the figure below:

Figure 1-9 ◀

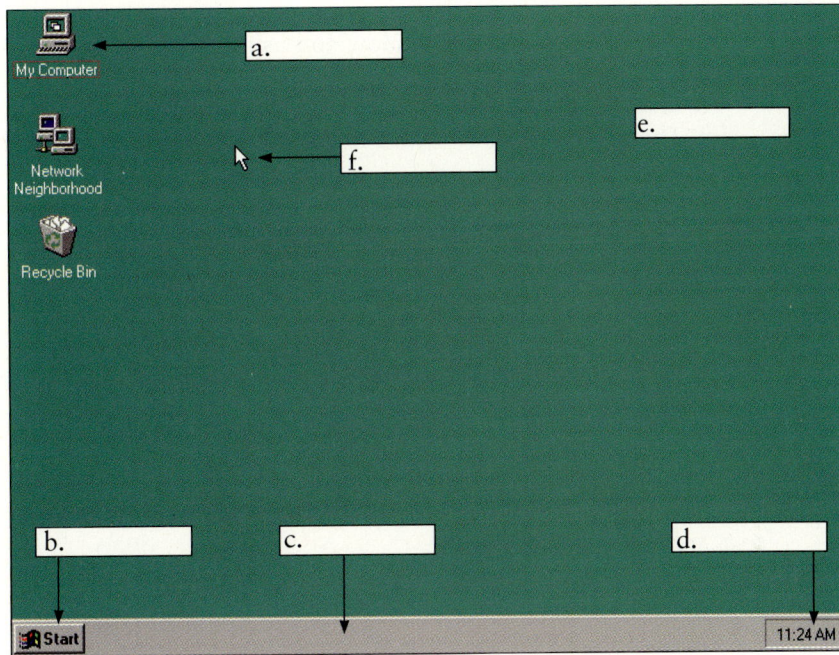

2. The _____ feature of Windows 95 allows you to run more than one program at a time.

3. The _____ is a list of options that provides you with access to programs, data, and configuration options.

4. What should you do if you are trying to move the pointer to the left edge of your screen, but your mouse runs into the keyboard?

5. Windows 95 shows you that an icon is selected by _____ it.

6. Even if you can't see a program, it might be running. How can you tell if a program is running?

7. Why is it good practice to close each program when you are finished using it?

8. Why do you need to shut down Windows 95 before you turn off your computer?

SESSION

1.2

In this session you will learn how to use many of the Windows 95 controls to manipulate windows and programs. You will learn how to change the size and shape of a window and to move a window so that you can customize your screen-based workspace. You will also learn how to use menus, dialog boxes, tabs, buttons, and lists to specify how you want a program to carry out a task.

Anatomy of a Window

When you run a program in Windows 95, it appears in a window. A **window** is a rectangular area of the screen that contains a program or data. A window also contains controls for manipulating the window and using the program. WordPad is a good example of how a window works.

Windows, spelled with an uppercase "W," is the name of the Microsoft operating system. The word "window" with a lowercase "w" refers to one of the rectangular windows on the screen.

To look at window controls:

1. Make sure Windows 95 is running and you are at the Windows 95 desktop screen.

2. Start WordPad.

> **TROUBLE?** To start WordPad, click the Start button, point to Programs, point to Accessories, and then click WordPad.

3. Make sure WordPad takes up the entire screen.

> **TROUBLE?** If WordPad does not take up the entire screen, click the ▢ button in the upper right corner.

4. On your screen, identify the controls labeled in Figure 1-10.

Figure 1-10 ◀
Window
controls

The **menu bar**
contains the
titles of menus,
such as File,
Edit, and Help.

The **toolbar**
contains buttons
that provide
you with a
shortcut to the
commands listed
on the menus.

The **status
bar** provides
you with
abbreviated
help relevant to
the task you
are doing.

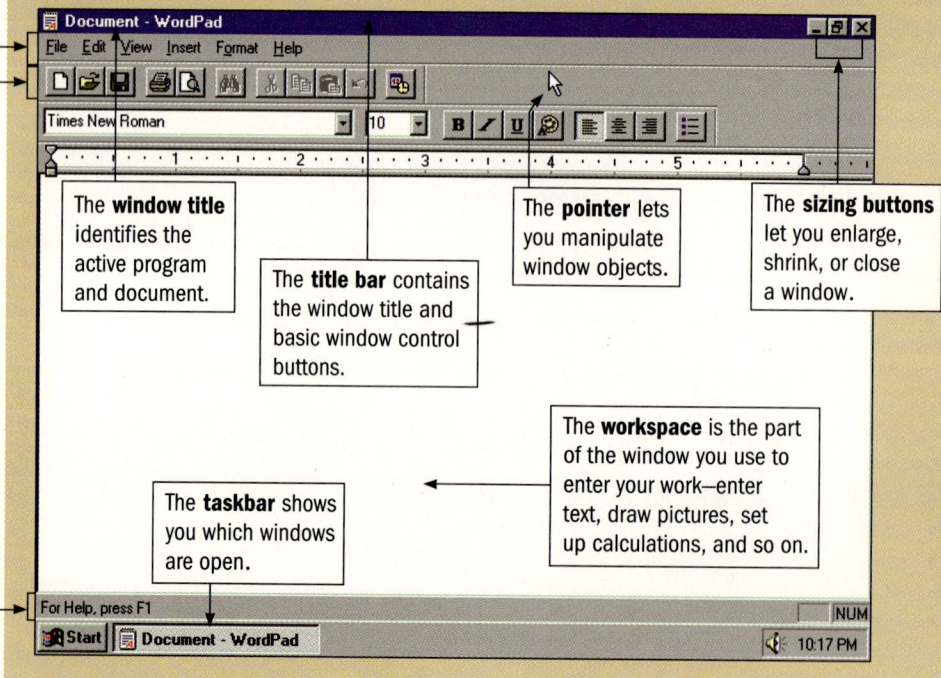

The **window title** identifies the active program and document.

The **title bar** contains the window title and basic window control buttons.

The **pointer** lets you manipulate window objects.

The **sizing buttons** let you enlarge, shrink, or close a window.

The **workspace** is the part of the window you use to enter your work—enter text, draw pictures, set up calculations, and so on.

The **taskbar** shows you which windows are open.

Manipulating a Window

There are three buttons located on the right side of the title bar. You are already familiar with the Close button. The Minimize button hides the window. The other button either maximizes the window or restores it to a predefined size. Figure 1-11 shows how these buttons work.

Figure 1-11
Minimize,
Maximize and
Restore buttons

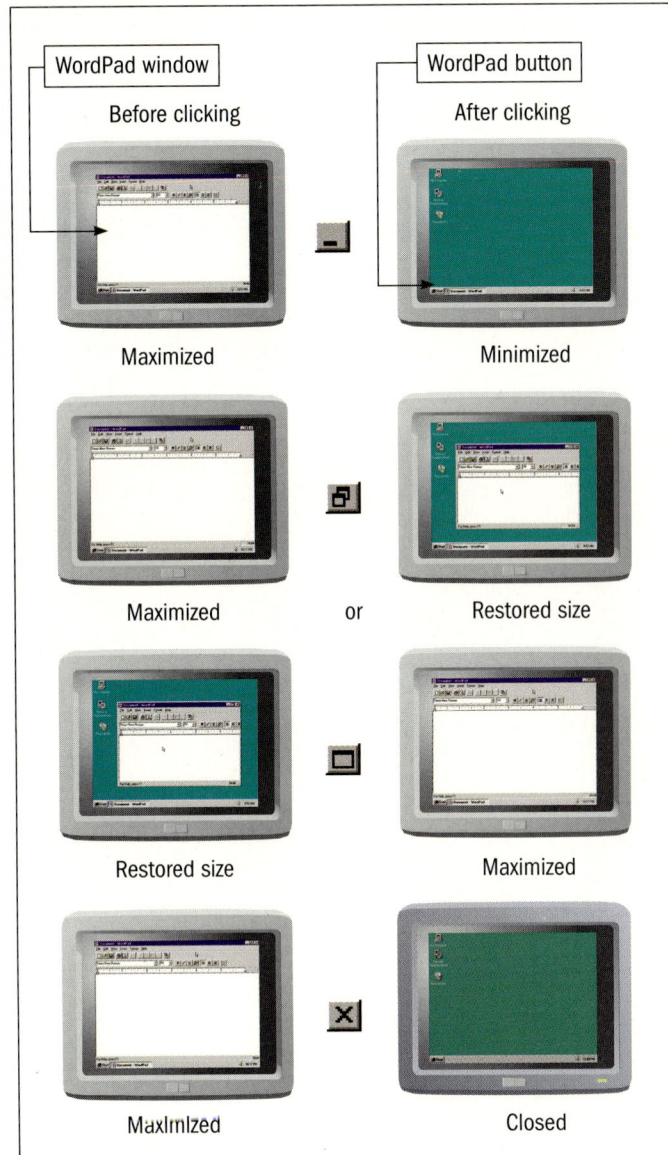

WordPad window
Before clicking

WordPad button
After clicking

Maximized   Minimized

The **Minimize button** shrinks the window, so you only see its button on the taskbar.

Maximized   or   Restored size

The middle button appears as a **Restore button** or a **Maximize button.** When the window is maximized, the Restore button appears. It can be used to reduce the size of the window to a predetermined or "normal" size. When the window does not fill the entire screen, the Maximize button appears. Clicking the Maximize button enlarges the window to fill the screen.

Restored size   Maximized

Maximized   Closed

The **Close button** closes the window and removes its button from the taskbar at the bottom of the screen.

Minimizing a Window

The **Minimize button** shrinks the current window so that only the button on the taskbar remains visible. You can use the Minimize button when you want to temporarily hide a window but keep the program running.

To minimize the WordPad window:

1. Click the **Minimize** button. The WordPad window shrinks so only the Document - WordPad button on the taskbar is visible.

   TROUBLE? If you accidentally clicked the Close button and closed the window, use the Start button to start WordPad again.

Redisplaying a Window

You can redisplay a minimized window by clicking the program's button on the taskbar. When you redisplay a window, it becomes the active window.

To redisplay the WordPad window:

1. Click the **Document - WordPad** button on the taskbar. The WordPad window is restored to its previous size. The Document - WordPad button looks pushed in as a visual clue that it is now the active window.

Restoring a Window

The **Restore** button 🗗 reduces the window so it is smaller than the entire screen. This is useful if you want to see more than one window at a time. Also, because of its small size, you can drag the window to another location on the screen or change its dimensions.

To restore a window:

1. Click the **Restore** button 🗗 on the WordPad title bar. The WordPad window will look similar to Figure 1-12, but the exact size of the window on your screen might be slightly different.

Figure 1-12 ◀
WordPad after clicking the Restore button

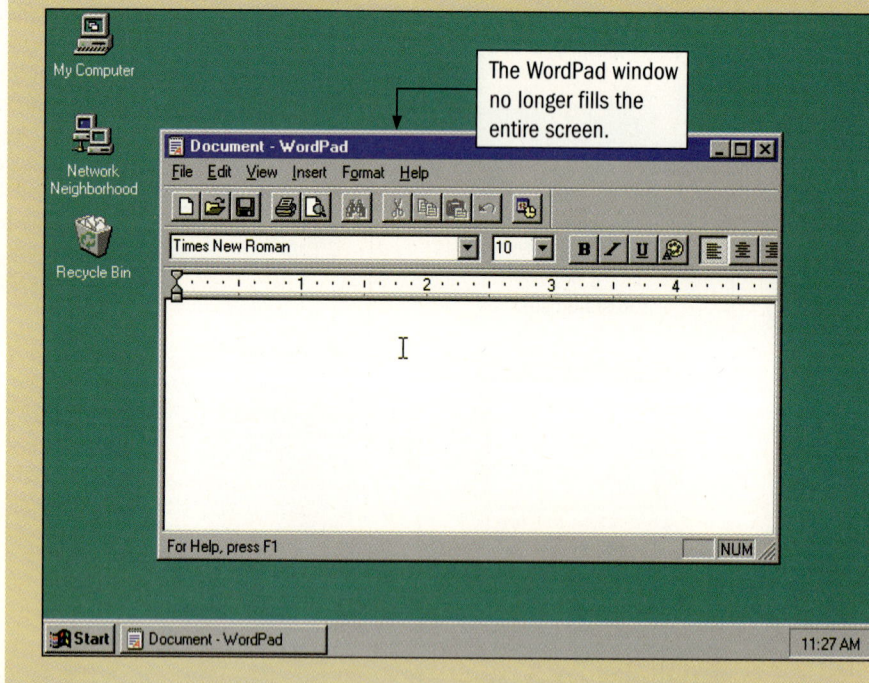

The WordPad window no longer fills the entire screen.

Moving a Window

You can use the mouse to **move** a window to a new position on the screen. When you hold down the mouse button while moving the mouse, it is called **dragging**. You can move objects on the screen by dragging them to a new location. If you want to move a window, you drag its title bar.

To drag the WordPad window to a new location:

1. Position the mouse pointer on the WordPad window title bar.

2. While you hold down the left mouse button, move the mouse to drag the window. A rectangle representing the window moves as you move the mouse.

3. Position the rectangle anywhere on the screen, then release the left mouse button. The WordPad window appears in the new location.

4. Now drag the WordPad window to the upper-left corner of the screen.

Changing the Size of a Window

3.1 NOTE

You can also change the size of a window by dragging the top, bottom, sides, and corners of the window, as you did in Windows 3.1.

You can also use the mouse to change the size of a window. Notice the sizing handle at the lower right corner of the window. The **sizing handle** provides a visible control for changing the size of a current window.

To change the size of the WordPad window:

1. Position the pointer over the sizing handle. The pointer changes to a diagonal arrow.

2. While holding down the mouse button, drag the sizing handle down and to the right.

3. Release the mouse button. Now the window is larger.

4. Practice using the sizing handle to make the WordPad window larger or smaller.

Maximizing a Window

The **Maximize button** enlarges a window so that it fills the entire screen. You will probably do most of your work using maximized windows because you can see more of your program and data.

To maximize the WordPad window:

1. Click the **Maximize** button on the WordPad title bar.

Using Program Menus

Most Windows programs use menus to provide an easy way for you to select program commands. The **menu bar** is typically located at the top of the program window and shows the titles of menus such as File, Edit, and Help.

Windows menus are relatively standardized—most Windows programs include similar menu options. It's easy to learn new programs, because you can make a pretty good guess about which menu contains the command you want.

Selecting Commands from a Menu

When you click any menu title, choices for that menu appear below the menu bar. These choices are referred to as **menu options**. To select a menu option, you click it. For example, the File menu is a standard feature in most Windows programs and contains the options related to working with a file: creating, opening, saving, and printing a file or document.

To select Print Preview from the File menu:

1. Click **File** in the WordPad menu bar to display the File menu.

TROUBLE? If you open a menu but decide not to select any of the menu options, you can close the menu by clicking its title again.

2. Click **Print Preview** to open the preview screen and view your document as it will appear when printed. This document is blank because you didn't enter any text.

3. After examining the screen, click the button labeled "Close" to return to your document.

Not all menu options immediately carry out an action—some show submenus or ask you for more information about what you want to do. The menu gives you hints about what to expect when you select an option. These hints are sometimes referred to as **menu conventions**. Study Figures 1-13a and 1-13b so you will recognize the Windows 95 menu conventions.

Figure 1-13a ◄
Menu
Conventions

Some menu options are toggle switches that can be either "on" or "off." When a feature is turned on, a **check mark** appears next to the menu option. When the feature is turned off, there is no check mark.

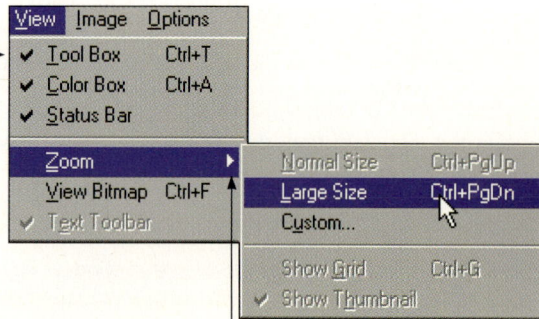

Certain menu selections lead you to an additional menu, called a **submenu**. A triangle on the right side of the menu choice indicates menu options that lead to submenus. When you move the pointer to a menu option with a triangle next to it, the submenu automatically appears.

Figure 1-13b ◄
Menu
conventions
(continued)

Some menu options are followed by a series of three dots, called an **ellipsis**. The dots indicate that you must make additional selections from a dialog box after you select that option. Options without dots do not require additional choices—they take effect as soon a you click them.

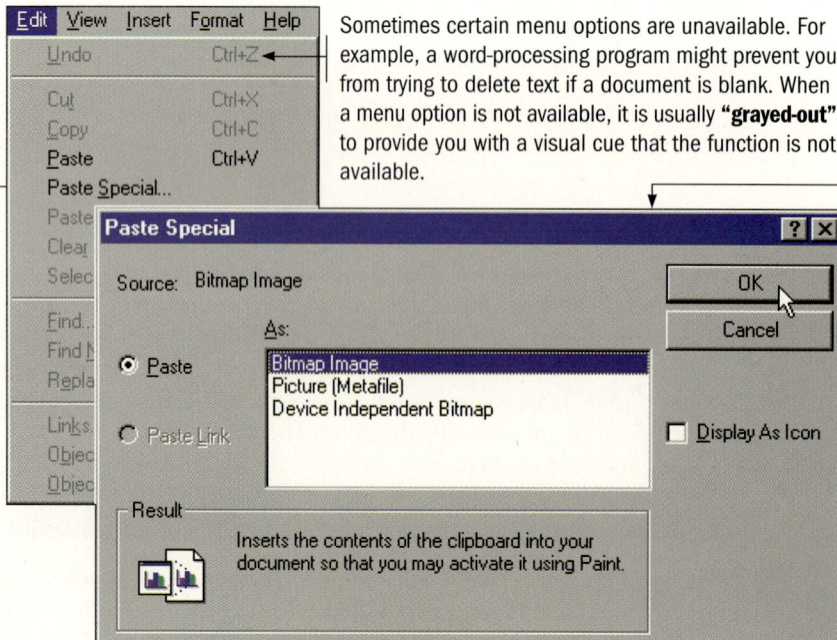

Sometimes certain menu options are unavailable. For example, a word-processing program might prevent you from trying to delete text if a document is blank. When a menu option is not available, it is usually **"grayed-out"** to provide you with a visual cue that the function is not available.

A **dialog box** lets you enter specification for how you want a task carried out.

Using Toolbars

A **toolbar** contains buttons that provide quick access to important program commands. Although you can usually perform all program commands using the menus, the toolbar provides convenient one-click access to frequently-used commands. For most Windows 95 functions, there is usually more than one way to accomplish a task. To simplify your introduction to Windows 95 in this tutorial, you will learn only one method for performing a task. As you become more accomplished using Windows 95, you can explore alternative methods.

In Session 1.1 you learned that Windows 95 programs include ToolTips that indicate the purpose and function of a tool. Now is a good time to explore the WordPad toolbar buttons by looking at their ToolTips.

To find out a toolbar button's function:

1. Position the pointer over any button on the toolbar, such as the Print Preview icon ⬚. After a short pause, the name of the button appears in a box and a description of the button appears in the status bar just above the Start button.

2. Move the pointer to each button on the toolbar to see its name and purpose.

You select a toolbar button by clicking it.

To select the Print Preview toolbar button:

1. Click the **Print Preview** button ⬚. The Print Preview dialog box appears. This is the same dialog box that appeared when you selected File, Print Preview from the menu bar.

2. Click ⬚ Close ⬚ to close the Print Preview dialog box.

Using List Boxes and Scroll Bars

As you might guess from the name, a **list box** displays a list of choices. In WordPad, date and time formats are shown in the Date/Time list box. List box controls include arrow buttons, a scroll bar, and a scroll box, as shown in Figure 1-14.

Figure 1-14 ◄
List box

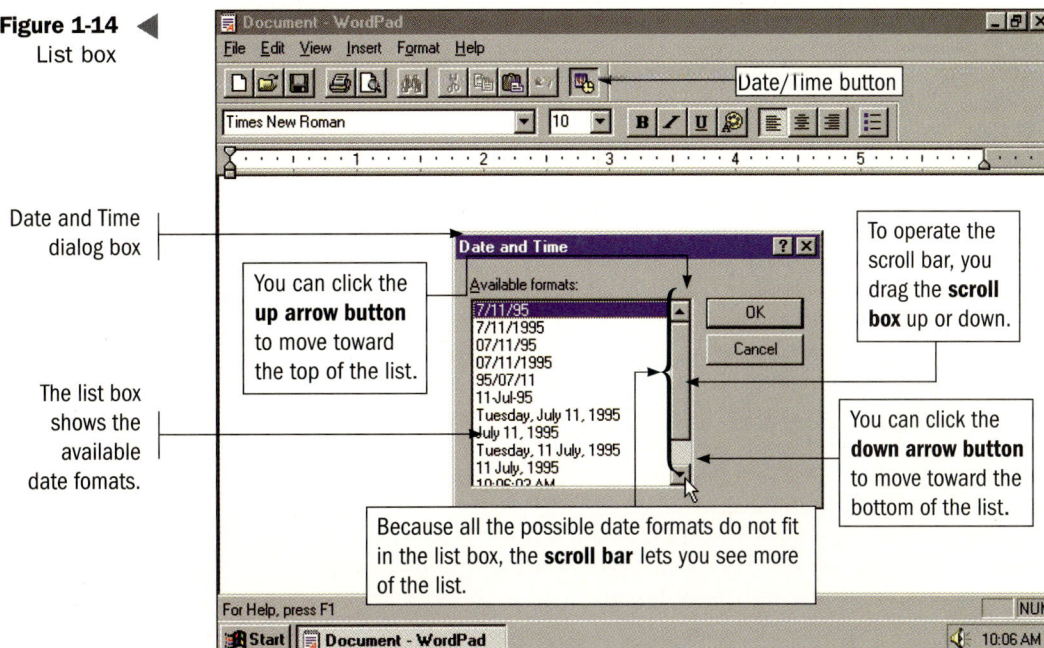

Date and Time dialog box

You can click the **up arrow button** to move toward the top of the list.

The list box shows the available date formats.

To operate the scroll bar, you drag the **scroll box** up or down.

You can click the **down arrow button** to move toward the bottom of the list.

Because all the possible date formats do not fit in the list box, the **scroll bar** lets you see more of the list.

To use the Date/Time list box:

1. Click the **Date/Time** button to display the Date and Time dialog box. See Figure 1-14.

2. To scroll down the list, click the **down arrow** button. See Figure 1-14.

3. Find the scroll box on your screen. See Figure 1-14.

4. Drag the **scroll box** to the top of the scroll bar. Notice how the list scrolls back to the beginning.

5. Find a date format similar to "October 2, 1997." Click that date format to select it.

6. Click the **OK** button to close the Date and Time list box. This inserts the current date in your document.

A variation of the list box, called a **drop-down list box**, usually shows only one choice, but can expand down to display additional choices on the list.

To use the Font Size drop-down list:

1. Click the **down arrow** button shown in Figure 1-15.

Figure 1-15 ◀
Type-size drop-down list box

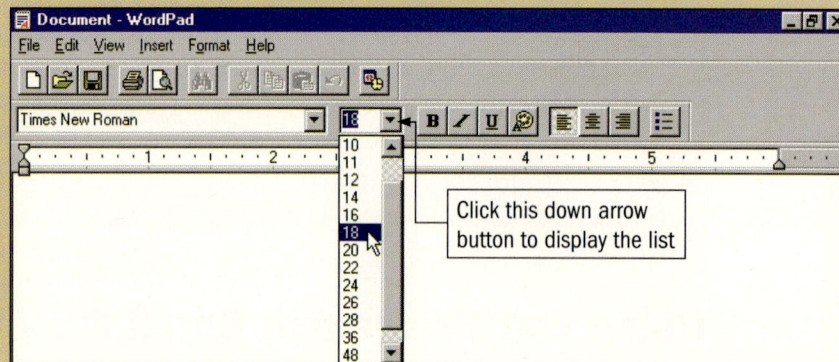

Click this down arrow button to display the list

2. Click **18**. The drop-down list disappears and the font size you selected appears at the top of the pull-down list.

3. Type a few characters to test the new font size.

4. Click the **down arrow** button in the Font Size drop-down list box again.

5. Click **12**.

6. Type a few characters to test this type size.

7. Click the **Close** button to close WordPad.

8. When you see the message "Save changes to Document?" click the **No** button.

Using Tab Controls, Radio Buttons, and Check Boxes

Dialog boxes often use tabs, radio buttons, or check boxes to collect information about how you want a program to perform a task. A **tab control** is patterned after the tabs on file folders. You click the appropriate tab to view different pages of information or choices. Tab controls are often used as containers for other Windows 95 controls such as list boxes, radio buttons, and check boxes.

Radio buttons, also called **option buttons**, allow you to select a single option from among one or more options. **Check boxes** allow you to select many options at the same time. Figure 1-16 explains how to use these controls.

Figure 1-16
Tabs, radio buttons, and check boxes

A **tab** indicates an "index card" that contains information or a group of controls, usually with related functions. To look at the functions on an index card, click the tab.

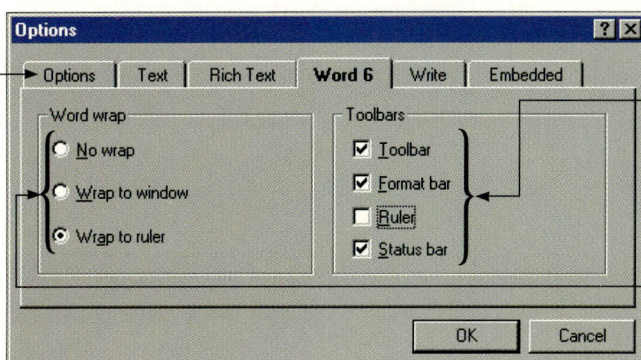

Check boxes allow you to select one or more options from a group. When you click a check box, a check mark appears in it. To remove a check mark from a box, click it again.

Radio buttons are round and usually come in groups of two or more. You can select only one radio button from a group. Your selection is indicated by a black dot.

Using Help

Windows 95 **Help** provides on-screen information about the program you are using. Help for the Windows 95 operating system is available by clicking the Start button on the taskbar, then selecting Help from the Start menu. If you want Help for a program, such as WordPad, you must first start the program, then use the Help menu at the top of the screen.

REFERENCE window

STARTING WINDOWS 95 HELP

- Click the Start button.
- Click Help.

To start Windows 95 Help:

1. Click the **Start** button.

2. Click **Help**.

Help uses tabs for each section of Help. Windows 95 Help tabs include Contents, Index, and Find as shown in Figure 1-17 on the following page.

Figure 1-17 ◀
Windows 95
Help

Each section of
Help is divided
into "books."
To open a book,
you click the
book, then click
the Open button.

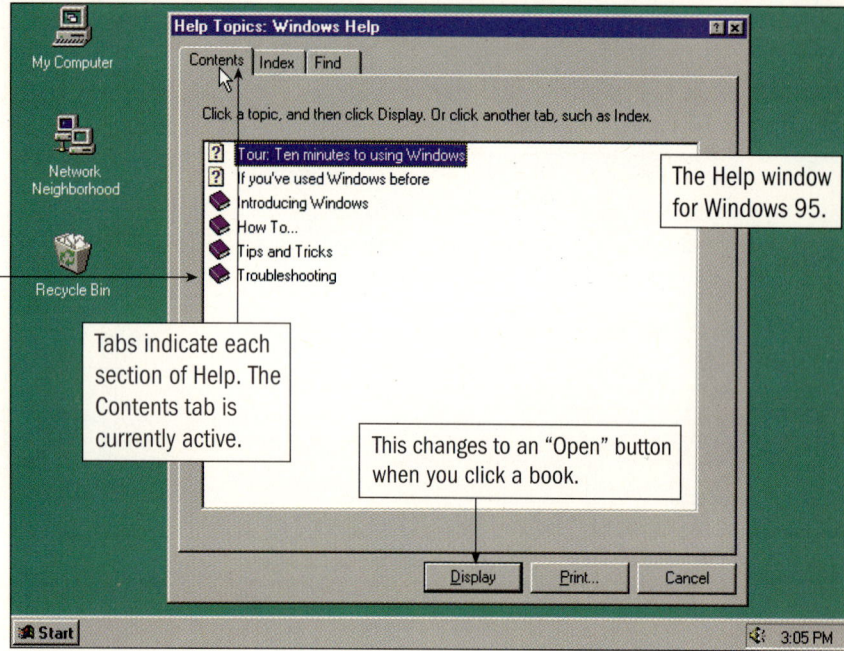

Tabs indicate each
section of Help. The
Contents tab is
currently active.

The Help window
for Windows 95.

This changes to an "Open" button
when you click a book.

The **Contents tab** groups Help topics into a series of books. You select a book, which then provides you with a list of related topics from which you can choose. The **Index tab** displays an alphabetical list of all the Help topics from which you can choose. The **Find tab** lets you search for any word or phrase in Help.

Suppose you're wondering if there is an alternative way to start programs. You can use the Contents tab to find the answer to your question.

To use the Contents tab:

1. Click the **Contents** tab to display the Contents window.

2. Click the **How To...** book title, then click the **Open** button. A list of related books appears below the book title. See. Figure 1-18.

Figure 1-18 ◀
Help window

Click this book,
then click the
Open button to
display a list of
related books.

Books related to
the "How To" topic.

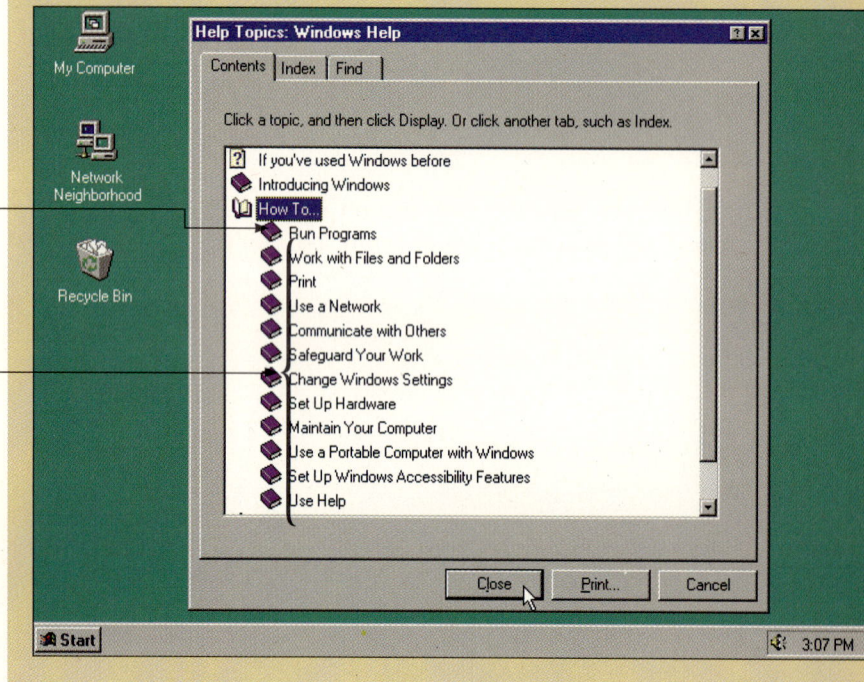

3. Click the **Run Programs** book, then click the **Open** button. The table of contents for this Help book is displayed.

4. Click the topic **Starting a Program**, then click the **Display** button. A Help window appears and explains how to start a program.

Help also provides you with definitions of technical terms. You can click any under-lined term to see its definition.

To see a definition of the term "taskbar":

1. Point to the underlined term, **taskbar** until the pointer changes to a hand. Then click.

2. After you have read the definition, click the definition to deselect it.

3. Click the **Close** button ☒ on the Help window.

The **Index tab** allows you to jump to a Help topic by selecting a topic from an indexed list. For example, you can use the Index tab to learn how to arrange the open windows on your desktop.

To find a Help topic using the Index tab:

1. Click the **Start** button.

2. Click **Help**.

3. Click the **Index** tab.

4. A long list of indexed Help topics appears. Drag the scroll box down to view additional topics.

5. You can quickly jump to any part of the list by typing the first few characters of a word or phrase in the line above the Index list. Type **desktop** to display topics related to the Windows 95 desktop.

6. Click the topic **arranging open windows on** in the bottom window.

7. Click the **Display** button as shown in Figure 1-19.

Figure 1-19 ◀
Displaying a
Help Topic

Click here to type
words or phrases.

Index topics are
displayed here.
Click the topic to
select it.

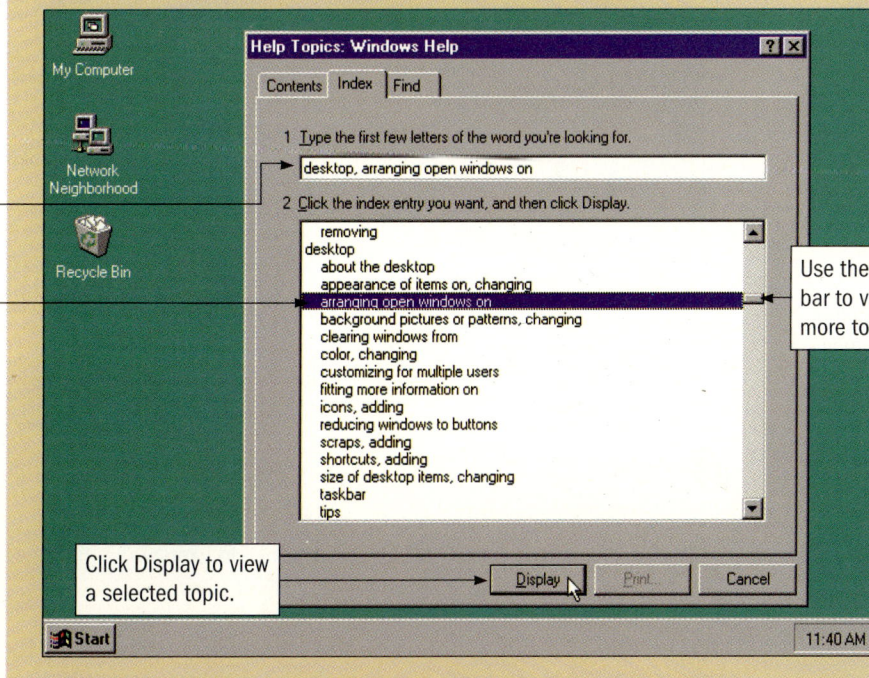

8. Click the **Close** button ☒ to close the Windows Help window.

The **Find tab** contains an index of all words in Windows 95 Help. You can use it to search for Help pages that contain a particular word or phrase. For example, suppose you heard that a screen saver blanks out your screen when you are not using it. You could use the Find tab to find out more about screen savers.

To find a Help topic using the Find tab:

1. Click the **Start** button ⊞ Start.

2. Click **Help**.

3. Click the **Find** tab.

TROUBLE? If the Find index has not yet been created on your computer, the computer will prompt you through several steps to create the index. Continue with Step 4 below after the Find index is created.

4. Type **screen** to display a list of all topics that start with the letters "screen."

5. Click **screen-saver** in the middle window to display the topics that contain the word "screen-saver."

6. Click **Having your monitor automatically turn off**, then click the **Display** button.

7. Click the **Help window** button shown in Figure 1-20. The screen saver is shown on a simulated monitor.

TROUBLE? If you see an error message, your lab does not allow students to modify screen savers. Click the OK button and go to Step 9.

Figure 1-20 ◀
Clicking a
Button in Help

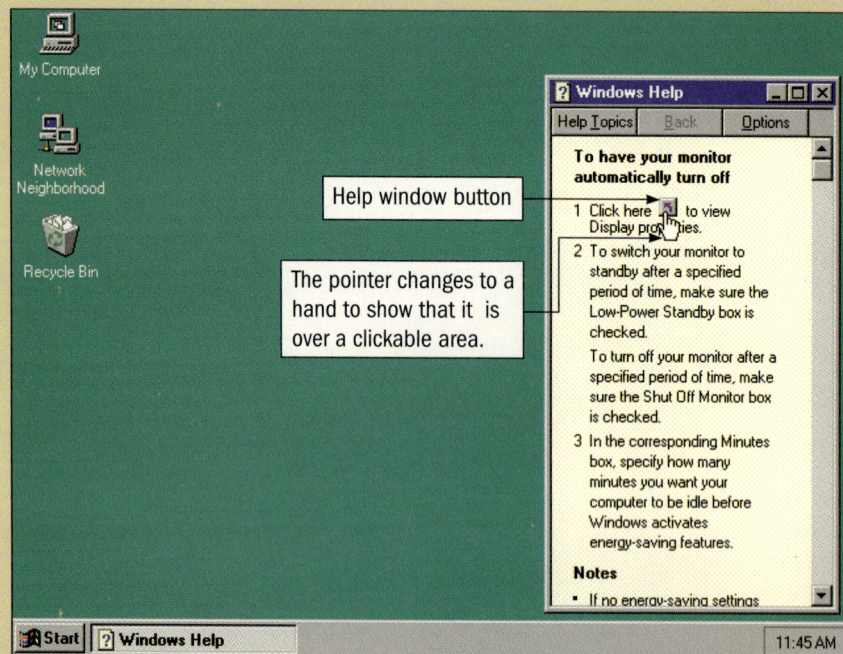

8. To close the Display properties window, click the **Close** button ☒ in the Display Properties window.

9. Click the **Close** button ☒ to close the Help window.

Now that you know how Windows 95 Help works, don't forget to use it! Use Help when you need to perform a new task or when you forget how to complete a procedure.

Quick Check

1 Label the parts of the window shown in Figure 1-21.

Figure 1-21 ◀

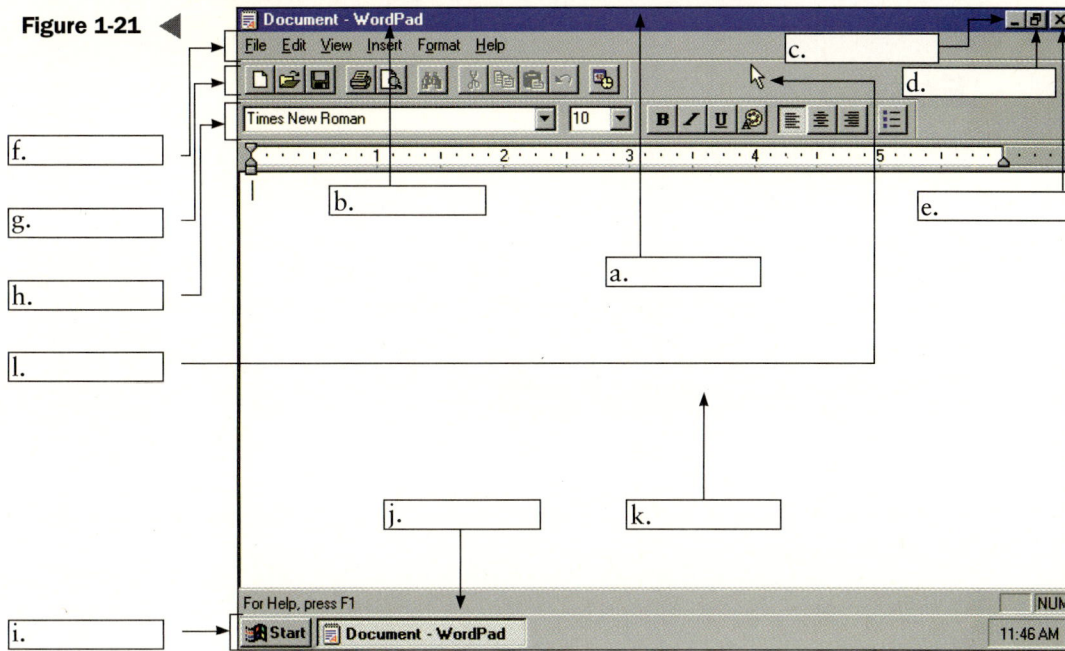

2 Provide the name and purpose of each button:
a. ▬
b. ▢
c. ▤
d. ✖

3 Explain each of the following menu conventions:
a. Ellipsis...
b. Grayed out
c. ▶
d. ✔

4 A(n) _____ consists of a group of buttons, each of which provides one-click access to important program functions.

5 Label each part of the dialog box below:

Figure 1-22 ◀

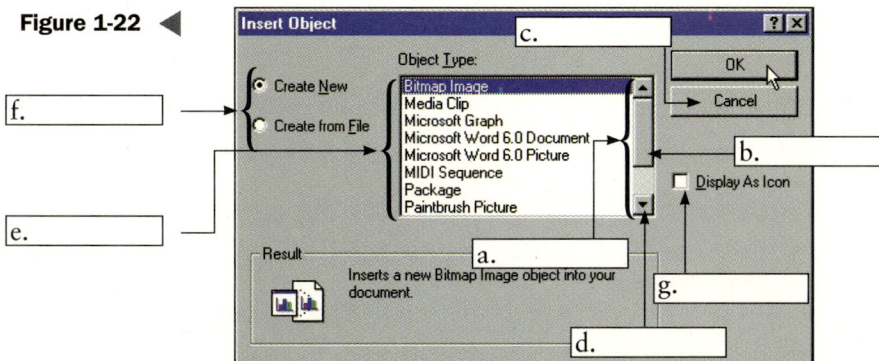

6 Radio buttons allow you to select _____ option(s) at a time, but _____ allow you to select one or more options.

7 It is a good idea to use _____ when you need to learn how to perform new tasks, simplify tedious procedures, and correct actions that did not turn out as you expected.

End Note

You've finished the tutorial, but Steve Laslow still hasn't returned. Take a moment to review what you have learned. You now know how to start a program using the Start button. You can run more than one program at a time and switch between programs using the buttons on the taskbar. You have learned the names and functions of window controls and Windows 95 menu conventions. You can now use toolbar buttons, list boxes, drop-down lists, radio buttons, check boxes, and scroll bars. Finally, you can use the Contents, Index, and Find tabs in Help to extend your knowledge of how to use Windows 95.

Tutorial Assignments

1. Running Two Programs and Switching Between Them In this tutorial you learned how to run more than one program at a time using WordPad and Paint. You can run other programs at the same time, too. Complete the following steps and write out your answers to questions b through f:

    a. Start the computer. Enter your user name and password if prompted to do so.
    b. Click the Start button. How many menu options are on the Start menu?
    c. Run the program Calculator program located on the Programs, Accessories menu. How many buttons are now on the taskbar?
    d. Run the Paint program and maximize the Paint window. How many application programs are running now?
    e. Switch to Calculator. What are the two visual clues that tell you that Calculator is the active program?
    f. Multiply 576 by 1457. What is the result?
    g. Close Calculator, then close Paint.

2. WordPad Help In Tutorial 1 you learned how to use Windows 95 Help. Just about every Windows 95 program has a help feature. Many computer users can learn to use a program just by using Help. To use Help, you would start the program, then click the Help menu at the top of the screen. Try using WordPad Help:

    a. Start WordPad.
    b. Click Help on the WordPad menu bar, then click Help Topics.
    c. Using WordPad help, write out your answers to questions 1 through 3.
        1. How do you create a bulleted list?
        2. How do you set the margins in a document?
        3. What happens if you hold down the Alt key and press the Print Screen key?
    d. Close WordPad.

3. Using Help to Explore Paint In this assignment, you will use the Paint Help to learn how to use the Paint program. Your goal is to create and print a picture that looks like the one in Figure 1-23.

Figure 1-23 ◄

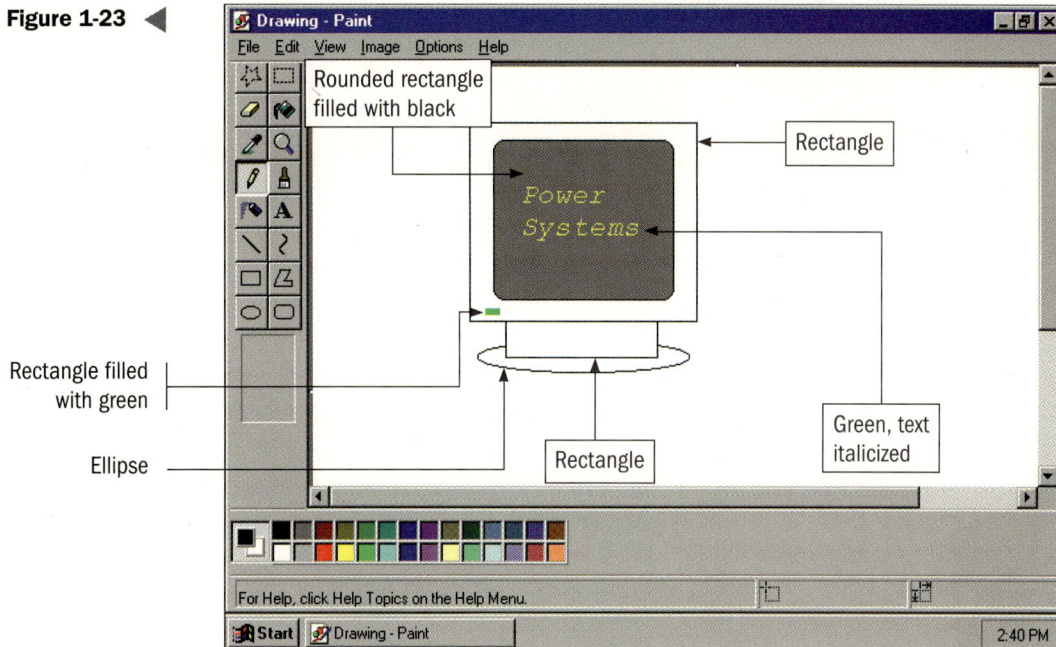

a. Start Paint.

b. Click Help, then click Help Topics.

c. Use Paint Help to learn how to put text in a picture and how to draw rectangles and circles.

d. Draw a picture of a monitor using rectangles, circles, and text as shown in Figure 1-23.

e. Print your picture.

f. Close Paint.

4. The Windows 95 Tutorial Windows 95 includes a five part on-line tutorial. In Tutorial 1 you learned about starting programs, switching windows, and using Help. You can use the on-line Windows 95 Tutorial to review what you learned and pick up some new tips for using Windows 95. Complete the following steps and write out your answers to questions f, g, and h:

a. Click the Start button to display the Start menu.

b. Click Help to display Windows help.

c. Click the Contents tab.

d. From the Contents screen, click Tour: Ten minutes to using Windows.

e. Click the Display button. If an error message appears, the Tour is probably not loaded on your computer. You will not be able to complete this assignment. Click Cancel, then click OK to cancel and check with your instructor or technical support person.

f. Click Starting a Program and complete the tutorial. What are the names of the seven programs on the Accessories menu in the tutorial?

g. Click Switching Windows and complete the on-line tutorial. What does the Minimize button do?

h. Click Using Help and complete the tutorial. What is the purpose of the [?] button?

i. Click the Exit button to close the Tour window.

j. Click the Exit Tour button to exit the Tour and return to the Windows 95 desktop.

Lab Assignments

Using a Keyboard

1. Learning to Use the Keyboard If you are not familiar with computer keyboards, you will find the Keyboard Lab helpful. This Lab will give you a structured introduction to special computer keys and their function in Windows 95. As you work through the Lab, you will be asked to answer Quick Check questions about what you have learned. At the end of the lab, you will see a summary report of your answers. If your instructor wants you to print out your answers to these questions, click the Print button on the summary report screen.

    a. Click the Start button.

    b. Point to Programs, then point to CTI Windows 95 Applications.

    c. Click Windows 95 New Perspectives Brief.

    d. Click Using a Keyboard. If you cannot find Windows 95 New Perspectives Brief or Using a Keyboard, ask for help from your instructor or technical support person.

Using a Mouse

2. Mouse Practice If you would like more practice using a mouse, you can complete the Mouse Lab. As you work through the Lab, you will be asked to answer Quick Check questions about what you have learned. At the end of the lab, the Quick Check Report shows you how you did. If your instructor wants you to print out your answers to these questions, click the Print button on the summary report screen.

    a. Click the Start button.

    b. Point to Programs, then point to CTI Windows 95.

    c. Point to Windows 95 New Perspectives Brief.

    d. Click Using a Mouse. If you cannot find Windows 95 New Perspectives Brief or Using a Mouse, ask for help from your instructor or technical support person.

Working with Files

OBJECTIVES

In this tutorial you will learn to:

■ Format a disk

■ Enter, select, insert, and delete text

■ Create and save a file

■ Open and edit a file

■ Print a file

■ Create a Student Disk

■ View the list of files on your disk

■ Move, copy, delete, and rename a file

■ Make a backup of your floppy disk

LABS

Using Files

CASE

Your First Day in the Lab—Continued

Steve Laslow is back from class, grinning. "I see you're making progress!"

"That's right," you reply. "I know how to run programs, control windows, and use Help. I guess I'm ready to work with my word-processing and spreadsheet software now."

Steve hesitates before he continues, "You could, but there are a few more things about Windows 95 that you should learn first."

Steve explains that most of the software you have on your computer—your word-processing, spreadsheet, scheduling, and graphing software—was created especially for the Windows 95 operating system. This software is referred to as **Windows 95 applications** or **Windows 95 programs**. You can also use software designed for Windows 3.1, but Windows 95 applications give you more flexibility. For example, when you name a document in a Windows 95 application, you can use descriptive filenames with up to 255 characters, whereas in Windows 3.1 you are limited to eight-character names.

You typically use Windows 95 applications to create files. A **file** is a collection of data that has a name and is stored in a computer. You typically create files that contain documents, pictures, and graphs when you use software packages. For example, you might use word-processing software to create a file containing a document. Once you create a file, you can open it, edit its contents, print it, and save it again—usually using the same application program you used to create it.

Another advantage of Windows 95 is that once you know how to save, open, and print files with one Windows 95 application, you can perform those same functions in *any* Windows 95 application. This is because Windows 95 applications have similar controls. For example, your word-processing and spreadsheet software will have identical menu commands to save, open, and print documents. Steve suggests that it would be worth a few minutes of your time to become familiar with these menus in Windows 95 applications.

You agree, but before you can get to work, Steve gives you one final suggestion: you should also learn how to keep track of the files on your disk. For instance, you might need to find a file you have not used for a while or you might want to delete a file if your disk is getting full. You will definitely want to make a backup copy of your disk in case something happens to the original. Steve's advice seems practical, and you're eager to explore these functions so you can get to work!

Tutorial 2 will help you learn how to work with Windows 95 applications and keep track of the files on your disk. When you've completed this tutorial, you'll be ready to tackle all kinds of Windows 95 software!

SESSION

2.1

In Session 2.1 you will learn how to format a disk so it can store files. You will create, save, open, and print a file. You will find out how the insertion point is different from the mouse pointer, and you will learn the basic skills for Windows 95 text entry, such as inserting, deleting, and selecting.

For this tutorial you will need two blank 3 ¹/₂-inch disks.

Formatting a Disk

Before you can save files on a disk, the disk must be formatted. When the computer **formats** a disk, the magnetic particles on the disk surface are arranged so data can be stored on the disk. Today, many disks are sold preformatted and can be used right out of the box. However, if you purchase an unformatted disk, or if you have an old disk that you want to completely erase and reuse, you can format the disk using the Windows 95 Format command.

The following steps tell you how to format a 3 ½-inch high-density disk using drive A. Your instructor will tell you how to revise the instructions given in these steps if the procedure is different for your lab equipment.

All data on the disk you format will be erased, so don't perform these steps using a disk that contains important files.

To format a disk:

1. Start Windows 95, if necessary.

2. Write your name on the label of a 3 ¹/₂-inch disk.

3. Insert your disk in drive A. See Figure 2-1.

Figure 2-1 ◀
Inserting a
disk into the
disk drive

floppy disk drive ———

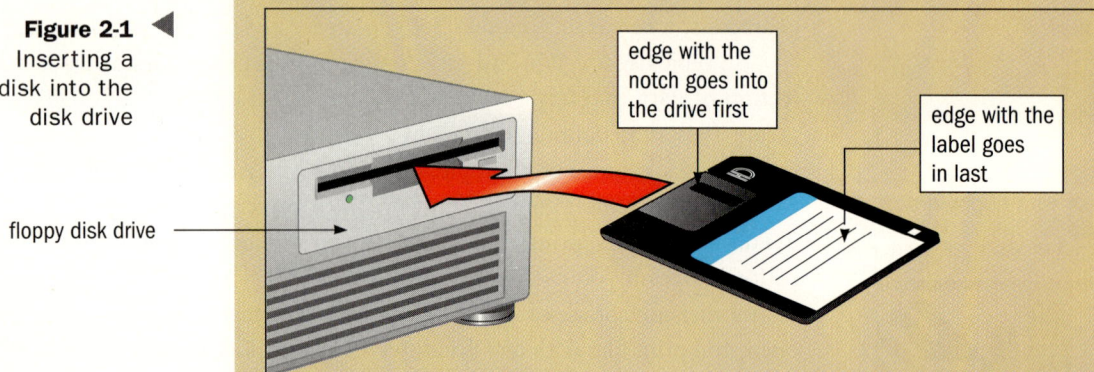

edge with the
notch goes into
the drive first

edge with the
label goes
in last

TROUBLE? If your disk does not fit in drive A, put it in drive B and substitute drive B for drive A in all of the steps for the rest of the tutorial.

4. Click the **My Computer** icon to select it, then press the **Enter** key. Make sure you can see the My Computer window. See Figure 2-2.

TROUBLE? If you see a list instead of icons like those in Figure 2-2, click View. Then click Large Icon.

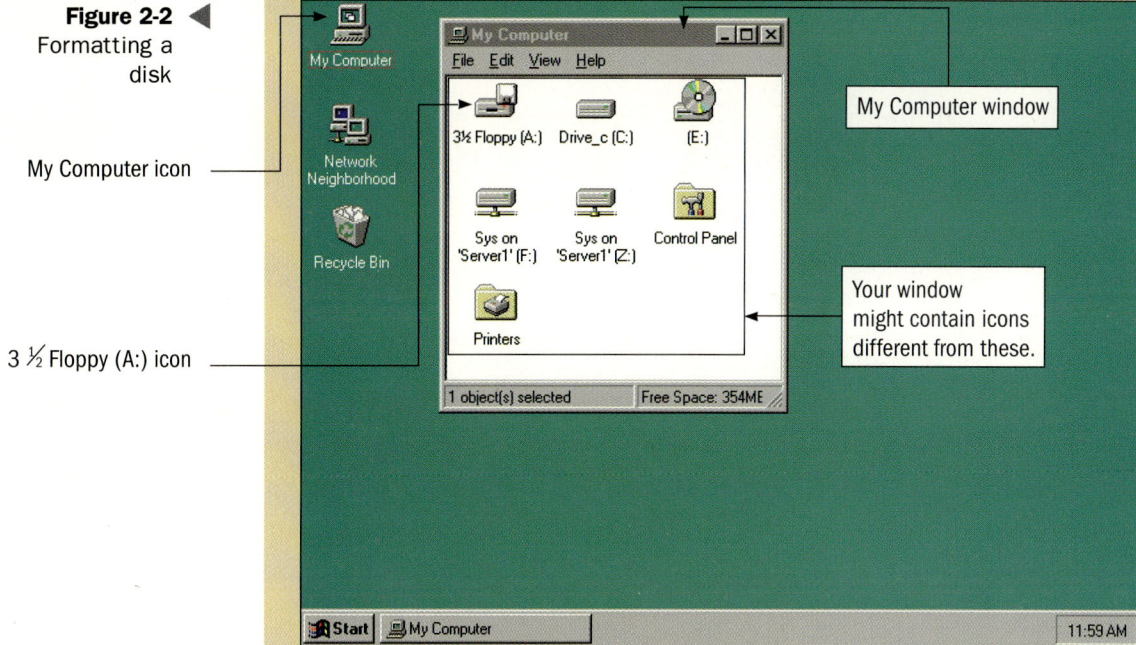

Figure 2-2 ◀
Formatting a
disk

My Computer icon

3 ½ Floppy (A:) icon

5. Click the **3 ½ Floppy (A:)** icon to select it.

6. Click **File** on the My Computer Window as shown in Figure 2-3.

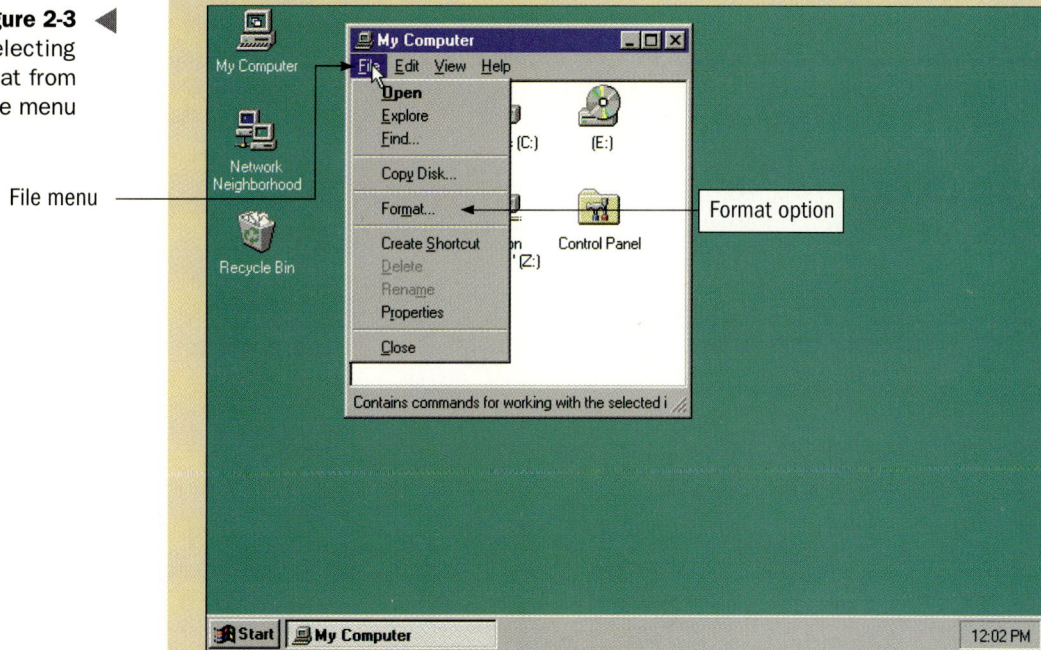

Figure 2-3 ◀
Selecting
Format from
the File menu

File menu

7. Click **Format** to open the Format dialog box.

8. Make sure the dialog box settings on your screen match those in Figure 2-4.

Figure 2-4 ◄
The Format
dialog box

Format type
is "Full."

Only the
Display box
contains a
check mark.

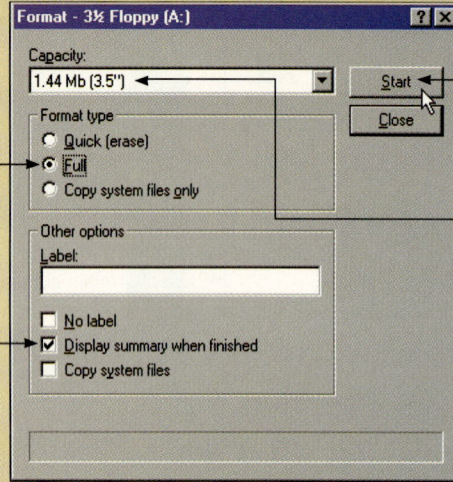

Start button
begins format

The capacity box
shows 1.44 Mb
(3.5").

9. On the right side of the dialog box is a Start button. Click this **Start** button to begin formatting the disk. A series of blue boxes at the bottom of the Format window show you how the format is progressing.

When the format is complete, the Format Results dialog box appears. See Figure 2-5.

Figure 2-5 ◄
The Format
Results dialog
box

Total disk
space

Total space available
to store data

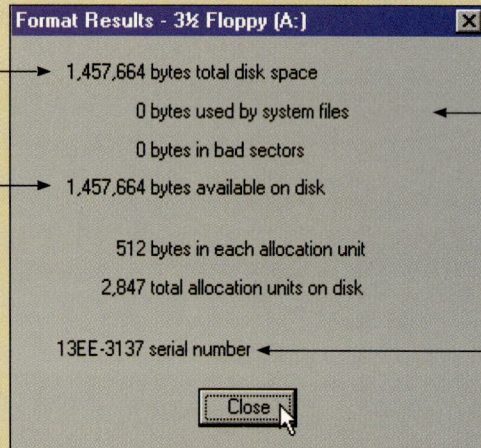

Bad sectors are
defects on the disk
surface—no data
will be stored in
these sectors.

Your serial number
might differ.

10. Click [Close].

11. Close all the windows on the desktop.

TROUBLE? To close the windows click each Close button [✕].

Working with Text

To accomplish many computing tasks, you need to type text in documents and text boxes. Windows 95 facilitates basic text entry by providing a text-entry area, by showing you where your text will appear on the screen, by helping you move around on the screen, and by providing insert and delete functions.

When you type sentences and paragraphs of text, do *not* press the Enter key when you reach the right margin. The software contains a feature called **word wrap** that automatically continues your text on the next line. Therefore, you should press Enter only when you have completed a paragraph.

If you type the wrong character, press the Backspace key to backup and delete the character. You can also use the Delete key. What's the difference between the Backspace and the Delete keys? The Backspace key deletes the character to left. The Delete key deletes the character to the right.

Now you will type some text using WordPad to learn about text entry.

To type text in WordPad:

1. Start WordPad.

   TROUBLE? If the WordPad window does not fill the screen, click the Maximize button ▣.

2. Notice the flashing vertical bar, called the **insertion point**, in the upper-left corner of the document window. The insertion point indicates where the characters you type will appear.

3. Type your name, using the Shift key to type uppercase letters and using the spacebar to type spaces, just like on a typewriter.

4. Press the **Enter** key to end the current paragraph and move the insertion point down to the next line.

5. As you type the following sentences, watch what happens when the insertion point reaches the right edge of the screen:

   This is a sample typed in WordPad. See what happens when the insertion point reaches the right edge of the screen.

   TROUBLE? If you make a mistake, delete the incorrect character(s) by pressing the Backspace key on your keyboard. Then type the correct character(s).

The Insertion Point versus the Pointer

The insertion point is not the same as the mouse pointer. When the mouse pointer is in the text-entry area, it is called the **I-beam pointer** and looks like I. Figure 2-6 explains the difference between the insertion point and the I-beam pointer.

Figure 2-6 ◀
The insertion point vs. the pointer

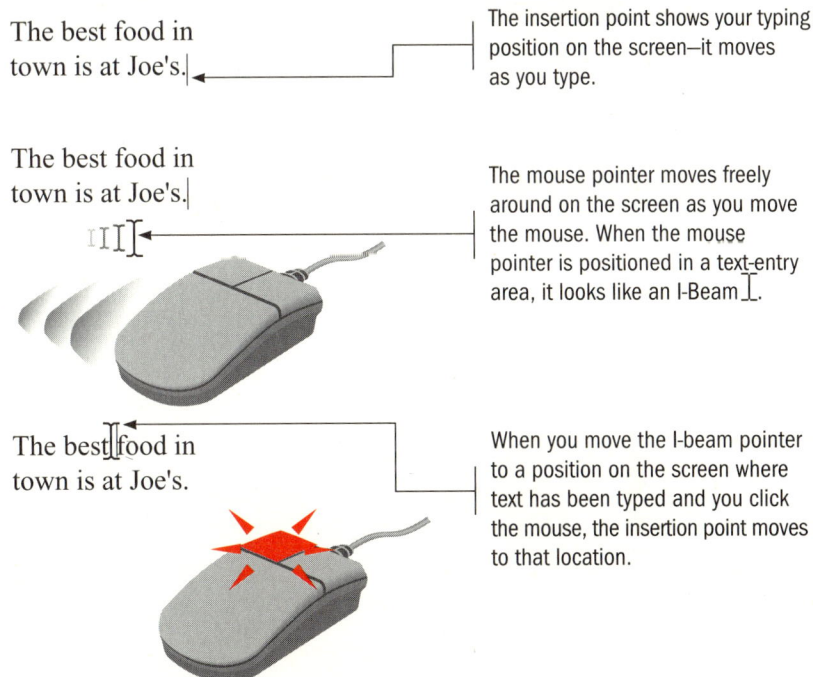

The best food in town is at Joe's.|

The insertion point shows your typing position on the screen—it moves as you type.

The best food in town is at Joe's.|

The mouse pointer moves freely around on the screen as you move the mouse. When the mouse pointer is positioned in a text-entry area, it looks like an I-Beam I.

The best food in town is at Joe's.

When you move the I-beam pointer to a position on the screen where text has been typed and you click the mouse, the insertion point moves to that location.

To move the insertion point:

1. Check the location of the insertion point and the I-beam pointer. The insertion point should be at the end of the sentence you typed in the last set of steps.

   TROUBLE? If you don't see the I-beam pointer, move your mouse until you see it.

2. Use the mouse to move the I-beam pointer to the word "sample," then click the left mouse button. The insertion point jumps to the location of the I-beam pointer.

3. Move the I-beam pointer to a blank area near the bottom of the work space and click the left mouse button. *Notice that the insertion point does not jump to the location of the I-beam pointer.* Instead the insertion point jumps to the end of the last sentence. The insertion point can move only within existing text. It cannot be moved out of the existing text area.

Selecting Text

Many text operations are performed on a **block** of text, which is one or more consecutive words, sentences, or paragraphs. Once you select a block of text, you can delete it, move it, replace it, underline it, and so on. As you select a block of text, the computer highlights it. If you want to remove the highlighting, just click in the margin of your document.

Suppose you want to replace the phrase "See what happens" with "You can watch word wrap in action." You do not have to delete the text one character at a time. Instead you can highlight the entire phrase and begin to type the replacement text.

To select and replace a block of text:

1. Move the I-beam pointer just to the left of the word "See."

2. While holding down the left mouse button, drag the I-beam pointer over the text to the end of the word "happens." The phrase "See what happens" should now be highlighted. See Figure 2-7.

Figure 2-7 ◄
Highlighting
text

Position the
I-beam pointer here.

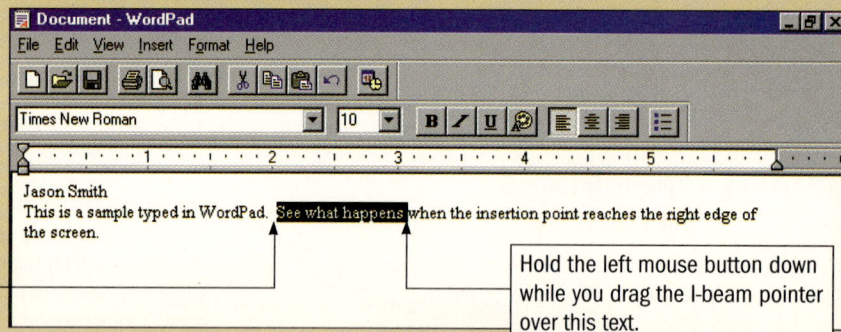

Hold the left mouse button down while you drag the I-beam pointer over this text.

3. Release the left mouse button.

   TROUBLE? If the phrase is not highlighted correctly, repeat Steps 1 through 3.

4. Type: **You can watch word wrap in action**

   The text you typed replaces the highlighted text. Notice that you did not need to delete the highlighted text before you typed the replacement text.

Inserting a Character

Windows 95 programs usually operate in **insert mode**—when you type a new character, all characters to the right of the cursor are pushed over to make room.

Suppose you want to insert the word "sentence" before the word "typed."

To insert characters:

1. Position the I-beam pointer just before the word "typed," then click.

2. Type: **sentence**.

3. Press the **spacebar**.

3.I NOTE

When you save a file with a long filename, Windows 95 also creates an eight-character filename that can be used by Windows 3.1 applications. The eight-character filename is created by using the first six non-space characters from the long filename, then adding a tilde (~) and a number. For example, the filename Car Sales for 1997 would be converted to Carsal~1.

Notice how the letters in the first line are pushed to the right to make room for the new characters. When a word gets pushed past the right margin, the word-wrap feature pushes it down to the beginning of the next line.

Saving a File

As you type text, it is held temporarily in the computer's memory. For permanent storage, you need to save your work on a disk. In the computer lab, you will probably save your work on a floppy disk in drive A.

When you save a file, you must give it a name. Windows 95 allows you to use filenames containing up to 255 characters, and you may use spaces and punctuation symbols. You cannot use the symbols \ ? : * " < > | in a filename, but other symbols such as &, -, and $ are allowed.

Most filenames have an **extension**. An **extension** is a suffix of up to three characters that is separated from the filename by a period, as shown in Figure 2-8.

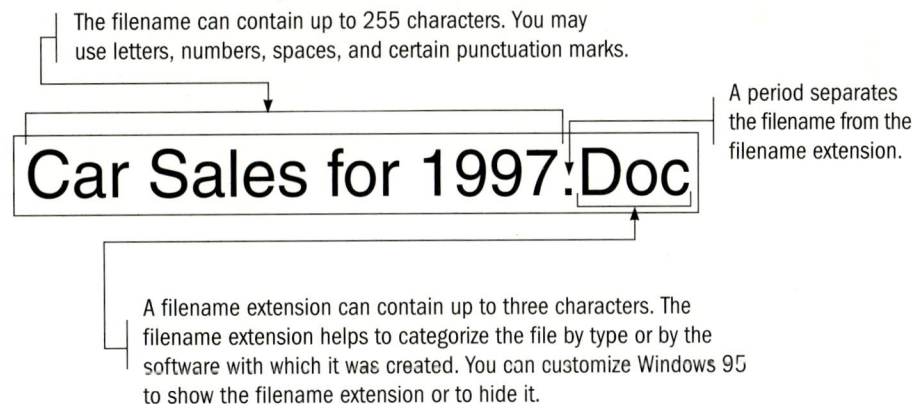

The filename can contain up to 255 characters. You may use letters, numbers, spaces, and certain punctuation marks.

A period separates the filename from the filename extension.

Car Sales for 1997.Doc

A filename extension can contain up to three characters. The filename extension helps to categorize the file by type or by the software with which it was created. You can customize Windows 95 to show the filename extension or to hide it.

Figure 2-8 ◀
Filename and extension

The file extension indicates which application you used to create the file. For example, files created with Microsoft Word software have a .Doc extension. In general, you will not add an extension to your filenames, because the application software automatically does this for you.

Windows 95 keeps track of file extensions, but does not always display them. The steps in these tutorials refer to files using the filename, but not its extension. So if you see the filename Sample Text in the steps, but "Sample Text.Doc" on your screen, don't worry—these are the same files.

Now you can save the document you typed.

To save a document:

1. Click the **Save** button 🖫 on the toolbar. Figure 2-9 shows the location of this button and the Save As dialog box that appears after you click it.

Figure 2-9 ◀
The Save button

Save button —

Save As
dialog box
appears after
you click the
Save button

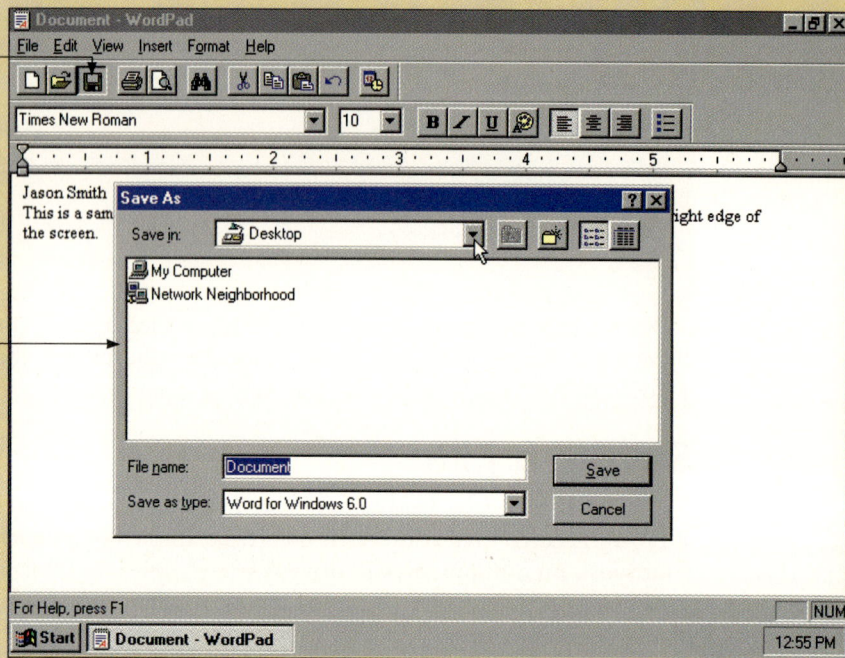

2. Click ▾ on the side of the Save in: box to display a list of drives. See Figure 2-10.

Figure 2-10 ◀
Selecting the
drive

3 ½ Floppy (A:)
drive menu
option

Down Arrow button
on the Save In box

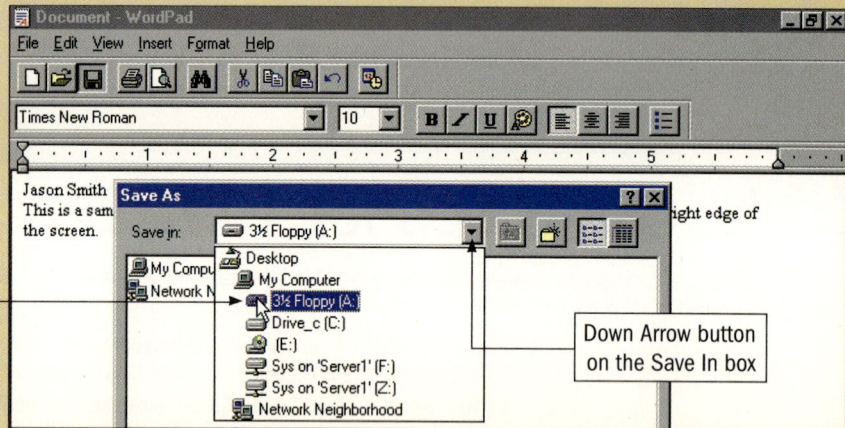

3. Click **3½ Floppy (A:)**.

4. Select the text in the File Name box.

TROUBLE? To select the text, position the I-beam pointer at the beginning of the word "Document." While you hold down the mouse button, drag the I-beam pointer to the end of the word.

5. Type **Sample Text** in the File Name box.

6. Click the **Save** button. Your file is saved on your Student Disk and the document title, "Sample Text," appears on the WordPad title bar.

What if you tried to close WordPad *before* you saved your file? Windows 95 would display a message—"Save changes to Document?" If you answer "Yes," Windows displays the Save As dialog box so you can give the document a name. If you answer "No," Windows 95 closes WordPad without saving the document.

After you save a file, you can work on another document or close WordPad. Since you have already saved your Sample Text document, you should continue this tutorial by closing WordPad.

To close WordPad:

1. Click the **Close** button ☒ to close the WordPad window.

Opening a File

Suppose you save and close the Sample Text file, then later you want to revise it. To revise a file you must first open it. When you **open** a file, its contents are copied into the computer's memory. If you revise the file, you need to save the changes before you close the application or work on a different file. If you close a revised file without saving your changes, you will lose the revisions.

Typically, you would use one of two methods to open a file. You could select the file from the Documents list or the My Computer window, or you could start an application program and then use the Open button to open the file. Each method has advantages and disadvantages. You will have an opportunity to try both methods.

The first method for opening the Sample Text file simply requires you to select the file from the Documents list or the My Computer window. With this method the document, not the application program, is central to the task; hence this method is sometimes referred to as *document-centric*. You only need to remember the name of your document or file—you do not need to remember which application you used to create the document.

The Documents list contains the names of the last 15 documents used. You access this list from the Start menu. When you have your own computer, the Documents list is very handy. In a computer lab, however, the files other students use quickly replace yours on the list.

If your file is not in the Documents list, you can open the file by selecting it from the My Computer window. Windows 95 starts an application program that you can use to revise the file, then automatically opens the file. The advantage of this method is its simplicity. The disadvantage is that Windows 95 might not start the application you expect. For example, when you select Sample Text, you might expect Windows 95 to start WordPad because you used WordPad to type the text of the document. Depending on the software installed on your computer system, however, Windows 95 might start the Microsoft Word application instead. Usually this is not a problem. Although the application might not be the one you expect, you can still use it to revise your file.

3.1 NOTE

Document-centric features are advertised as an advantage of Windows 95. But you can still successfully use the application-centric approach you used with Windows 3.1 by opening your application, then opening your document.

To open the Sample Text file by selecting it from My Computer:

1. Click the **My Computer** icon. Press the **Enter** key. The My Computer window opens.

2. Click the **3½ Floppy (A:)** icon, then press the **Enter** key. The 3½ Floppy (A:) window opens.

TROUBLE? If the My Computer window disappears when you open the 3½ floppy (A:) window, click View, click Options, then click the Folder tab, if necessary. Click the radio button labelled "Browse Folders using a separate window for each folder." Then click the OK button.

3. Click the **Sample Text** file icon, then press the **Enter** key. Windows 95 starts an application program, then automatically opens the Sample Text file.

TROUBLE? If Windows 95 starts Microsoft Word instead of WordPad, don't worry. You can use Microsoft Word to revise the Sample Text document.

Now that Windows 95 has started an application and opened the Sample Text file, you could make revisions to the document. Instead, you should close all the windows on your desktop so you can try the other method for opening files.

To close all the windows on the desktop:

1. Click ☒ on each of the windows.

   TROUBLE? If you see a message, "Save changes to Document?" click the No button.

The second method for opening the Sample Text file requires you to open WordPad, then use the Open button to select the Sample Text file. The advantage of this method is that you can specify the application program you want to use—WordPad in this case. This method, however, involves more steps than the method you tried previously.

To start WordPad and open the Sample Text file using the Open button:

1. Start WordPad.

2. Click the **Open** button 📂 on the toolbar. Figure 2-11 shows the location of this button and the dialog box that appears after you click it.

Figure 2-11 ◄
The Open button
and dialog box

Open button ─────

Open dialog box ─────

Down Arrow button for
the Look in box

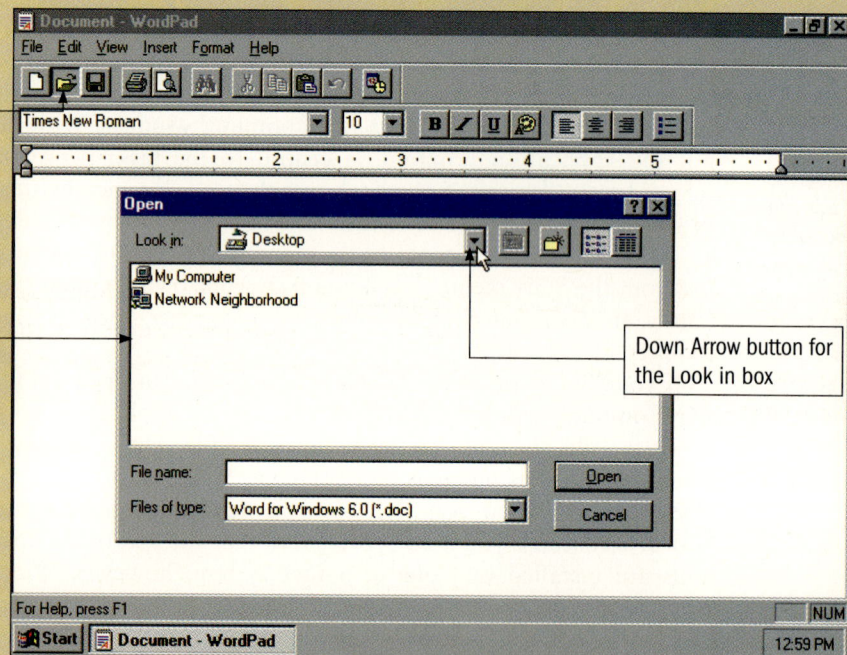

3. Click ▼ on the side of the Look in: box to display a list of drives. See Figure 2-11.

4. Click **3½ Floppy (A:)** from the list. See Figure 2-12.

5. Click **Sample Text** to make sure it is highlighted. See Figure 2-12.

Figure 2-12 ◀
Opening the
Sample Text file

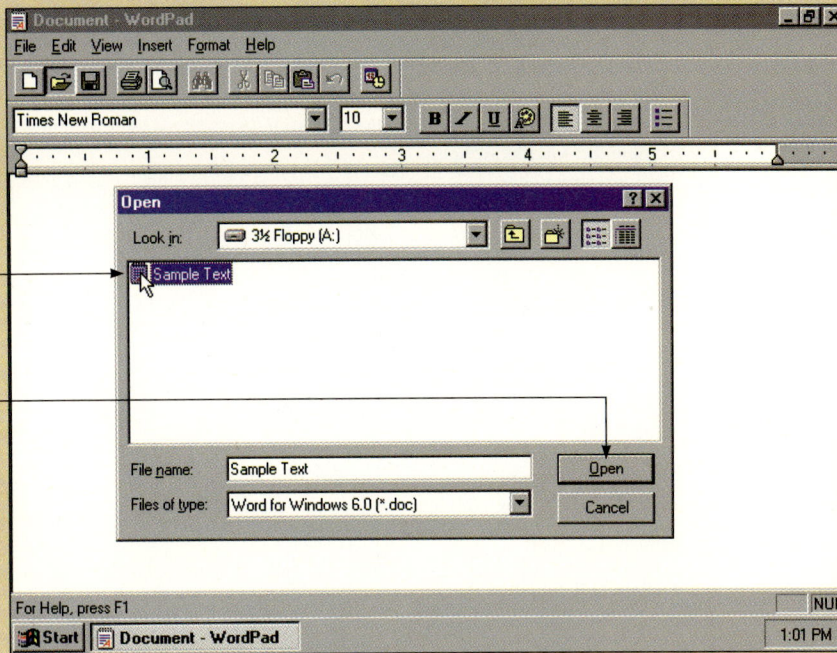

Sample Text
icon

Open button

6. Click [Open] in the lower right corner of the dialog box. Your document should appear in the WordPad work area.

Printing a File

Now that the Sample Text file is open, you can print it. It is a good idea to use Print Preview before you send your document to the printer. **Print Preview** shows on screen exactly how your document will appear on paper. You can check your page layout so you don't waste paper printing a document that is not quite the way you want it. Your instructor or technical support person might supply you with additional instructions for printing in your school's computer lab.

To preview, then print the Sample Text file:

1. Click the **Print Preview** button 🔍 on the toolbar.

2. Look at your print preview. Before you print the document and use paper, you should make sure that the font, margins, and other document features look the way you want them to.

   TROUBLE? If you can't read the document text on screen, click the Zoom In button.

3. Click the **Print** button. A Print dialog box appears.

4. Study Figure 2-13 to familiarize yourself with the controls in the Print dialog box.

This is the name of the printer that Windows 95 will use for this printout. If you are using a network, you might have a choice of printers. If you need to select a different printer, ask your instructor or your technical support person for help.

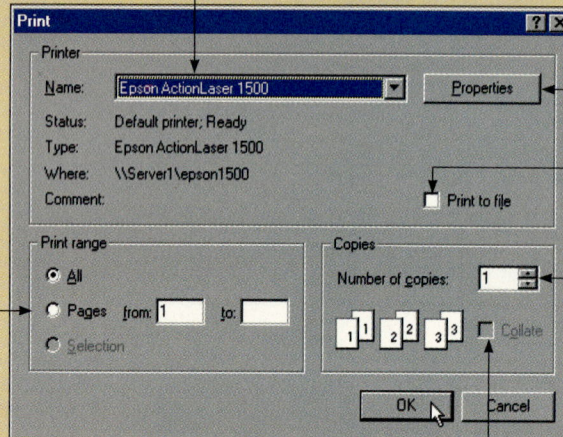

The Properties button lets you modify the way your printer is set up. Do not change any of the settings on your school printer without the consent of your instructor or technical support person.

When you click this check box, your printout will go on your disk instead of to the printer.

You can specify how many copies you want by typing the number in this box. Alternatively, you can use the arrow buttons to increase or decrease the number in the box.

Figure 2-13 ◀
The Print
dialog box

In the Print range box, you specify how much of the document you want to print. If you want to print only part of a document, click the Pages radio button and then enter the starting and ending pages for the printout.

Print		? X
Printer		
Name:	Epson ActionLaser 1500 ▼	Properties
Status:	Default printer; Ready	
Type:	Epson ActionLaser 1500	
Where:	\\Server1\epson1500	
Comment:		☐ Print to file
Print range		**Copies**
⦿ All		Number of copies: 1 ⏶⏷
○ Pages from: 1 to:		1 2 3 ☐ Collate
○ Selection		
	OK	Cancel

If you print more than one copy of a multi-page document, you can specify that you want the printout collated, so you don't have to collate the pages manually.

5. Make sure your screen shows the Print range set to "All" and the number of copies set to "1."

6. Click the **OK** button to print your document. If a message appears telling you printing is complete, click the **OK** button.

TROUBLE? If your document does not print, make sure the printer has paper and the printer on-line light is on. If your document still doesn't print, ask your instructor or technical support person for help.

7. Close WordPad.

TROUBLE? If you see the message "Save changes to Document?" click the "No" button.

Quick Check

1 A(n) _____ is a collection of data that has a name and is stored on a disk or other storage medium.

2 _____ erases all the data on a disk and arranges the magnetic particles on the disk surface so the disk can store data.

3 When you are working in a text box, the pointer shape changes to a(n) _____.

4 The _____ shows you where each character you type will appear.

5 _____ automatically moves text down to the beginning of the next line when you reach the right margin.

6 Explain how you select a block of text: _____.

7 Which of these characters are not allowed in Windows 95 file names: \ ? : * " < > | ! @ # $ % ^ & ; + - ( ) /

8 In the filename New Equipment.Doc, .Doc is a(n) ——————.

9 Suppose you created a graph using the Harvard Graphics software and then you stored the graph on your floppy disk under the name Projected 1997 Sales - Graph. The next day, you use Harvard Graphics to open the file and change the graph. If you want the new version of the file on your disk, you need to ——————.

10 You can save —————— by using the Print Preview feature.

SESSION

2.2

In this session, you will learn how to manage the files on your disk—a skill that can prevent you from losing important documents. You will learn how to list information about the files on your disk; organize the files into folders; and move, delete, copy, and rename files.

Creating Your Student Disk

For this session of the tutorial, you must create a Student Disk that contains some sample files. *You can use the disk you formatted in the previous session.*

If you are using your own computer, the CTI Windows 95 Applications menu selection will not be available. Before you proceed, you must go to your school's computer lab and find a computer that has the CTI Windows 95 Applications installed. Once you have made your own Student Disk, you can use it to complete this tutorial on any computer you choose.

To add the sample files to your Student Disk:

1. Write "Windows 95 Student Disk" on the label of your formatted disk.

2. Place the disk in Drive A.

   TROUBLE? If your 3½-inch disk drive is B, place your formatted disk in that drive instead, and for the rest of this session substitute Drive B where ever you see Drive A.

3. Click the **Start** button [🚩Start]. See Figure 2-14.

Figure 2-14 ◄
Making your
Student Disk

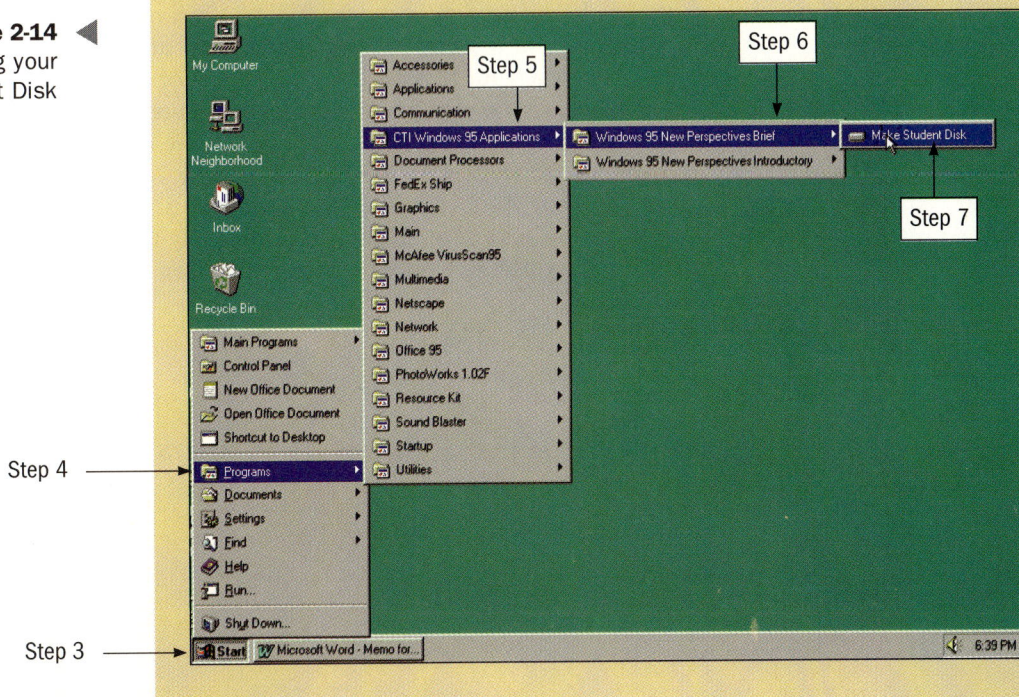

4. Point to **Programs.**

5. Point to **CTI Windows 95 Applications.**

TROUBLE? If CTI Windows 95 Applications is not listed, contact your instructor or technical support person.

6. Point to **Windows 95 New Perspectives Brief.**

7. Select **Make Student Disk.**

A dialog box opens, asking you to indicate the drive that contains your formatted disk.

8. If it is not already selected, click the Drive radio button that corresponds to the drive containing your student disk.

9. Click the **OK** button.

The sample files are copied to your formatted disk. A message tells you when all the files have been copied.

10. Click **OK.**

11. If necessary, close all the open windows on your screen.

Your Student Disk now contains sample files that you will use throughout the rest of this tutorial.

My Computer

The **My Computer** icon represents your computer, its storage devices, and its printers. The My Computer icon opens into the My Computer window, which contains an icon for each of the storage devices on your computer. On most computer systems the My Computer window also contains Control Panel and Printers folders, which help you add printers, control peripheral devices, and customize your Windows 95 work environment. Figure 2-15 on the following page explains more about the My Computer window.

You can use the My Computer window to keep track of where your files are stored and to organize your files. In this section of the tutorial you will move and delete files on your Student Disk in drive A. If you use your own computer at home or computer at work, you would probably store your files on drive C, instead of drive A. However, in a school lab environment you usually don't know which computer you will use, so you need to carry your files with you on a floppy disk that you use in drive A. In this session, therefore, you will learn how to work with the files on drive A. Most of what you learn will also work on your home or work computer when you use drive C.

In this session you will work with several icons, including My Computer. As a general procedure, when you want to open an icon, you click it and then press the Enter key.

Figure 2-15 ◄
Information
about My
Computer

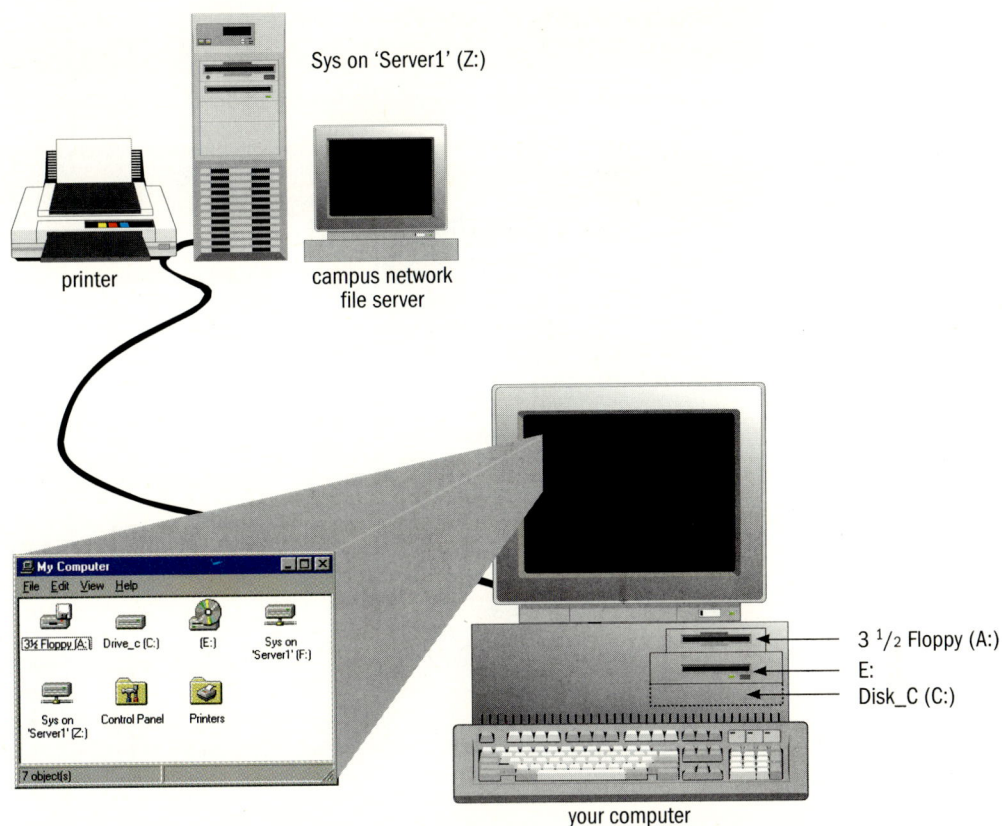

Sys on 'Server1' (Z:)

printer

campus network
file server

3 ¹/₂ Floppy (A:)

E:

Disk_C (C:)

your computer

My Computer
File Edit View Help

3½ Floppy [A:]   Drive_c (C:)   [E:]   Sys on 'Server1' (F:)

Sys on 'Server1' (Z:)   Control Panel   Printers

7 object(s)

REFERENCE window

OPENING AN ICON

■ Click the icon you want to open.
■ Press the Enter key.

Now you should open the My Computer icon.

To open the My Computer icon:

1. Click the **My Computer** icon to select it.

2. Press the **Enter** key. The My Computer window opens.

Now that you have opened the My Computer window, you can find out what is on your Student Disk in drive A.

To find out what is on your Student Disk:

1. Open the **3½ Floppy (A:)** icon by clicking it, then pressing the **Enter** key. A window appears showing the contents of drive A:. See Figure 2-16.

Figure 2-16 ◀
Contents of
Student Disk

Icons show contents
of drive A

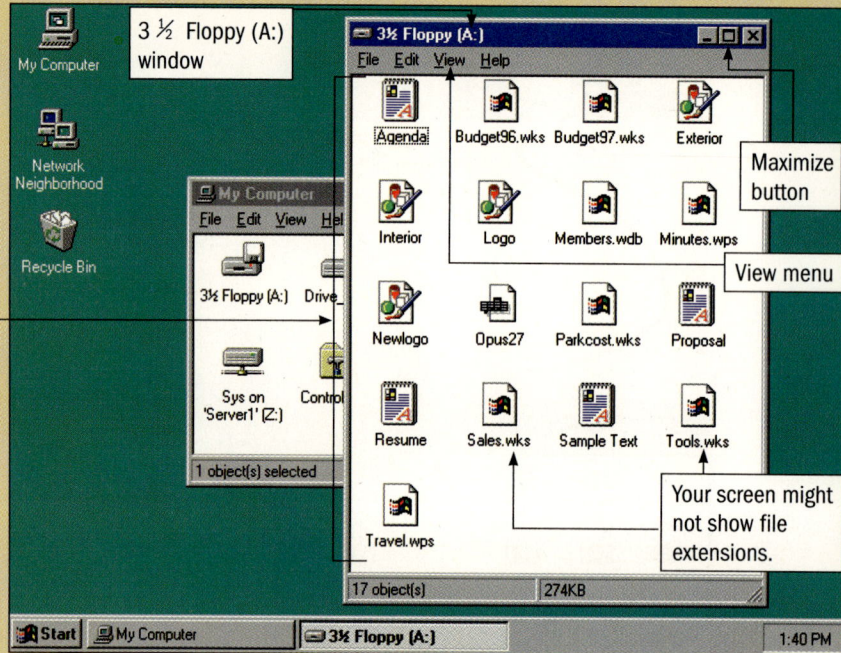

TROUBLE? If you see a list of file names instead of icons, click View, then click Large icons.

2. Click the **Maximize** button 🔲 if the window is not maximized.

Windows 95 provides four ways to view the contents of a disk—large icons, small icons, list, or details. The standard view, shown on your screen, displays a large icon and title for each file. The icon provides a visual cue to the type and contents of the file, as Figure 2-17 illustrates.

Figure 2-17 ◀
Program and
file icons

Text files that you can open and read using the WordPad or NotePad software are represented by notepad icons.

WordPad Document   Netlog   Exchng32

The icons for Windows programs usually depict an object related to the function of the program. For example, an icon that looks like a calculator signifies the Windows Calc program; an icon that looks like a computer signifies the Windows Explorer program.

Explorer   Calc

Many of the files you create are represented by page icons. Here the page icon for the Circles file shows some graphics tools to indicate the file contains a graphic. The Page icon for the Access file contains the Windows logo, indicating that Windows does not know if the file contains a document, graphics, or data base.

Access.mdb   Circles

Folders provide a way to group and organize files. A folder icon contains other icons for folders and files. Here, the System folder contains files used by the Windows operating system.

System

Non-Windows programs are represented by this icon of a blank window.

Command

The **Details** view shows more information than the large icon, small icon, and list views. Details view shows the file icon, the filename, the file size, the application you used to create the file, and the date/time the file was created or last modified.

To view a detailed list of files:

1. Click **View** then click **Details** to display details for the files on your disk as shown in Figure 2-18.

Figure 2-18 ◀
Detailed file list

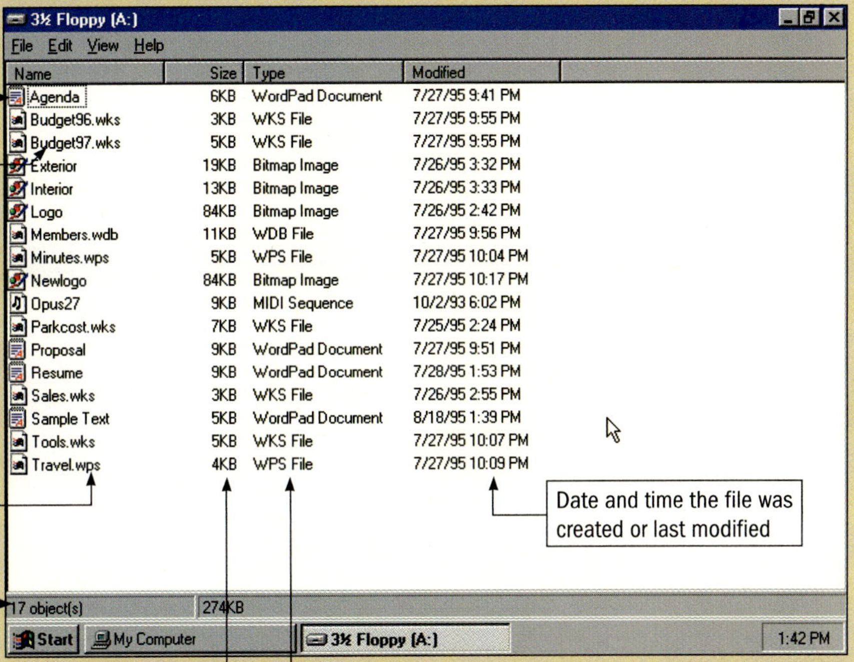

File icon ——————

Filename ——————

Your screen might not
show file extensions

Total number of
files and folders
in the window

Name	Size	Type	Modified
Agenda	6KB	WordPad Document	7/27/95 9:41 PM
Budget96.wks	3KB	WKS File	7/27/95 9:55 PM
Budget97.wks	5KB	WKS File	7/27/95 9:55 PM
Exterior	19KB	Bitmap Image	7/26/95 3:32 PM
Interior	13KB	Bitmap Image	7/26/95 3:33 PM
Logo	84KB	Bitmap Image	7/26/95 2:42 PM
Members.wdb	11KB	WDB File	7/27/95 9:56 PM
Minutes.wps	5KB	WPS File	7/27/95 10:04 PM
Newlogo	84KB	Bitmap Image	7/27/95 10:17 PM
Opus27	9KB	MIDI Sequence	10/2/93 6:02 PM
Parkcost.wks	7KB	WKS File	7/25/95 2:24 PM
Proposal	9KB	WordPad Document	7/27/95 9:51 PM
Resume	9KB	WordPad Document	7/28/95 1:53 PM
Sales.wks	3KB	WKS File	7/26/95 2:55 PM
Sample Text	5KB	WordPad Document	8/18/95 1:39 PM
Tools.wks	5KB	WKS File	7/27/95 10:07 PM
Travel.wps	4KB	WPS File	7/27/95 10:09 PM

Date and time the file was
created or last modified

17 object(s)   274KB

Start   My Computer   3½ Floppy (A:)   1:42 PM

File size (1 KB is equal
to about 1000 characters.)

File type or application used to create the file. File types might
differ depending on what software is installed on your computer.

2. Look at the file sizes. Do you see that **Logo** and **Newlogo** are the largest files?

3. Look at the dates and times that the files were modified. Which is the oldest file?

Now that you have looked at the file details, switch back to the large icon view.

To switch to the large icon view:

1. Click **View** then click **Large Icons** to return to the large icon display.

Folders and Directories

A list of files is referred to as a **directory**. The main directory of a disk is sometimes called the **root directory**. The root directory is created when you format a disk and is shown in parentheses at the top of the window. For example, at the top of your screen you should see "3 ½ Floppy (A:)." The root directory is A:. In some situations, the root directory is indicated by a backslash after the drive letter and colon, such as A:\. All of the files on your Student Disk are currently in the root directory.

If too many files are stored in a directory, the directory list becomes very long and difficult to manage. A directory can be divided into **folders** (also called **subdirectories**), into which you group similar files. The directory of files for each folder then becomes much shorter and easier to manage. For example, you might create a folder for all the papers you write for an English 111 class as shown in Figure 2-19.

A folder appears on the screen as a folder icon. When you open the folder icon, the folder is represented by a window. The ENG111 folder appears as the ENG111 window on the screen. The contents of the folder are represented by icons in the window.

Figure 2-19 ◀
Folders and directories

You create folders to hold groups of similar objects, such as documents, programs, and other folders.

A folder can contain other folders. Here, the ENG111 folder contains a folder called TERM PAPER.

If you open a folder that is contained in a window, it opens to its own window and displays the objects it contains.

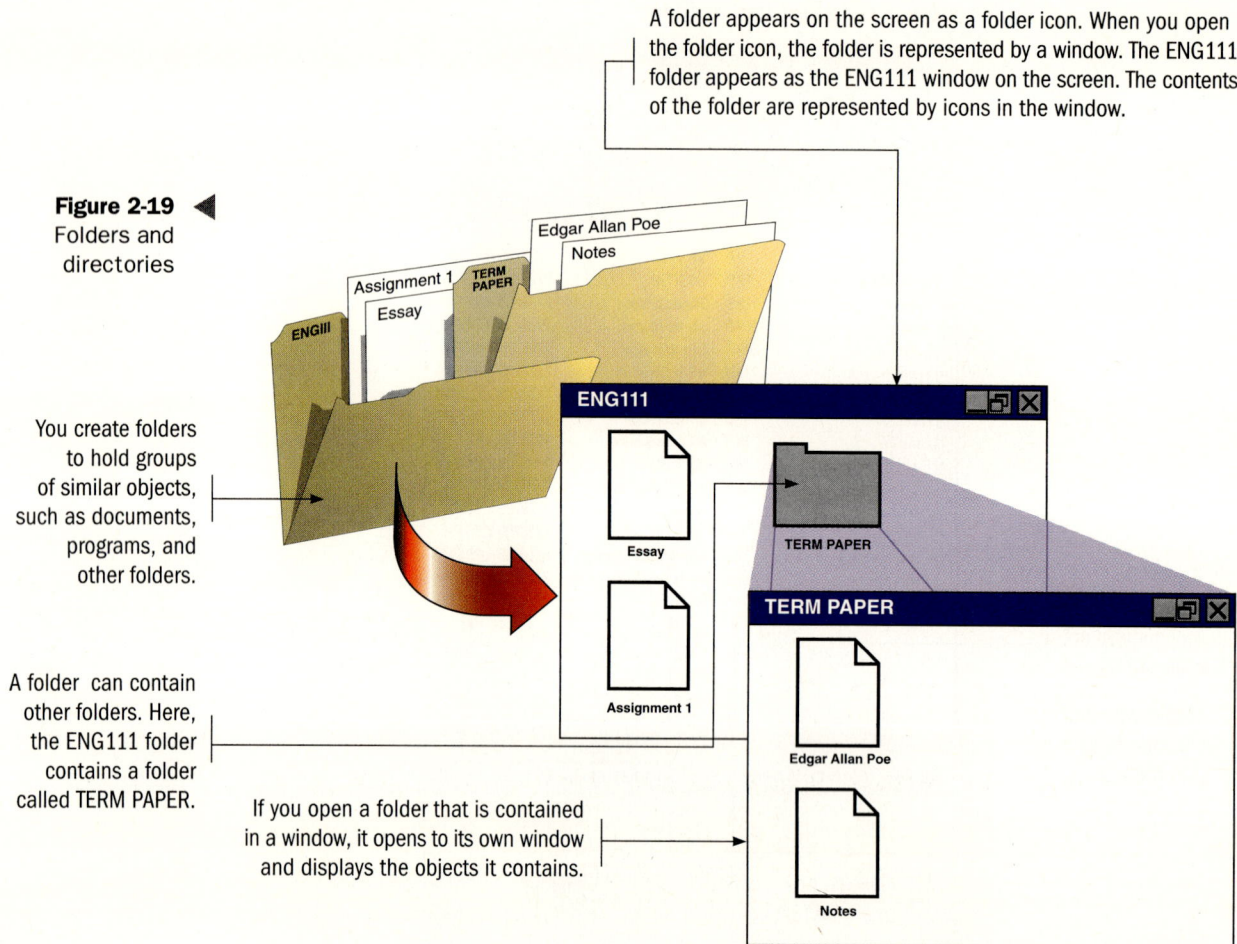

Now, you'll create a folder called My Documents to hold your document files.

To create a My Documents folder:

1. Click **File** then point to **New** to display the submenu.

2. Click **Folder**. A folder icon with the label "New Folder" appears.

3. Type **My Documents** as the name of the folder.

4. Press the **Enter** key.

When you first create a folder, it doesn't contain any files. In the next set of steps you will move a file from the root directory to the My Documents folder.

REFERENCE
window

CREATING A NEW FOLDER

- Open the My Computer icon to display the My Computer window.
- Open the icon for the drive on which you want to create the folder.
- Click File then point to New.
- From the submenu click Folder.
- Type the name for the new folder.
- Press the Enter key.

Moving and Copying a File

You can move a file from one directory to another or from one disk to another. When you move a file it is copied to the new location you specify, then the version in the old location is erased. The move feature is handy for organizing or reorganizing the files on your disk by moving them into appropriate folders. The easiest way to move a file is to hold down the *right* mouse button and drag the file from the old location to the new location. A menu appears and you select Move Here.

You can also copy a file from one directory to another, or from one disk to another. When you copy a file, you create an exact duplicate of an existing file in whatever disk or folder you specify. To copy a file from one folder to another on your floppy disk, you use the same procedure as for moving a file, except that you select Copy Here from the menu.

Suppose you want to move the Minutes file from the root directory to the My Documents folder. Depending on the software applications installed on your computer, this file is either called Minutes or Minutes.wps. In the steps it is referred to simply as Minutes.

To move the Minutes file to the My Documents folder:

1. Click the **Minutes** icon to select it.

2. Press and hold the right mouse button while you drag the **Minutes** icon to the My Documents folder. See Figure 2-20.

Figure 2-20 ◀
Moving a file

Minutes file ⟶

My Documents folder ⟶

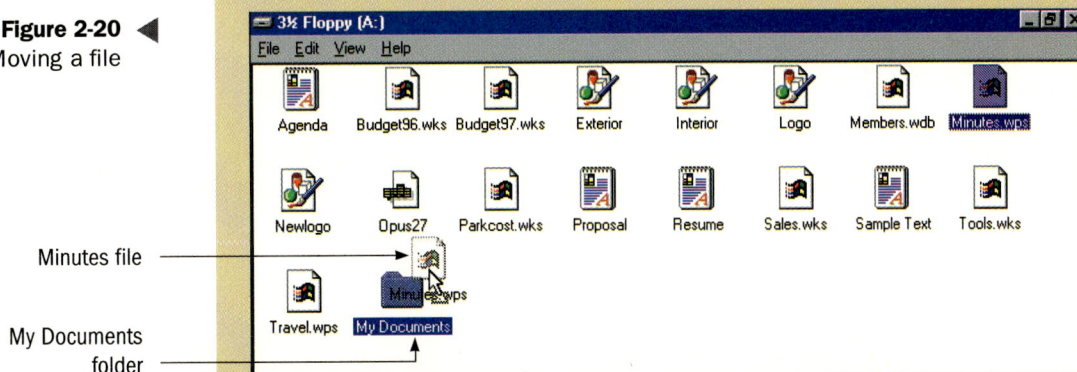

3. Release the right mouse button. A menu appears.

4. Click **Move Here**. A short animation shows the Minutes file being moved to My Documents. The Minutes icon disappears from the window showing the files in the root directory.

> **REFERENCE window**
>
> ## MOVING A FILE
>
> - Open the My Computer icon to display the My Computer window.
> - If the document you want to move is in a folder, open the folder.
> - Hold down the *right* mouse button while you drag the file icon to its new folder or disk location.
> - Click Move Here.
> - If you want to move more than one file at a time, hold down the Ctrl key while you click the icons for all the files you want to move.

3.1 NOTE

Windows 3.1 users be careful! When you delete or move an icon in the Windows 95 My Computer window you are actually deleting or moving the file. This is quite different from the way the Windows 3.1 Program Manager worked.

Anything you do to an icon in the My Computer window is actually done to the file represented by that icon. If you move an icon, the file is moved; if you delete an icon, the file is deleted.

After you move a file, it is a good idea to make sure it was moved to the correct location. You can easily verify that a file is in its new folder by displaying the folder contents.

To verify that the Minutes file was moved to My Documents:

1. Click the **My Documents** folder, then press **Enter**. The My Documents window appears and it contains one file—Minutes.

2. Click the My Documents window **Close** button ⊠.

   TROUBLE? If the My Computer window is no longer visible, click the My Computer icon, then press Enter. You might also need to open the 3 ½ Floppy (A:) icon.

Deleting a File

You delete a file or folder by deleting its icon. However, be careful when you delete a *folder*, because you also delete all the files it contains! When you delete a file from the hard drive, the filename is deleted from the directory but the file contents are held in the Recycle Bin. If you change your mind and want to retrieve the deleted file, you can recover it by clicking the Recycle Bin.

When you delete a file from a floppy disk, it does not go into the Recycle Bin. Instead it is deleted as soon as its icon disappears. Try deleting the file named Agenda from your Student Disk. Because this file is on the floppy disk and not on the hard disk, it will not go into the Recycle Bin.

To delete the file Agenda:

1. Click the icon for the file **Agenda**.

2. Press the **Delete** key.

3. If a message appears asking, "Are sure you want to delete Agenda?", click **Yes**. An animation, which might play too quickly to be seen, shows the file being deleted.

<table>
<tr><td rowspan="2">REFERENCE
window</td><td>DELETING A FILE</td></tr>
<tr><td>■ Click the icon for the file you want to delete.
■ Press the Delete key.</td></tr>
</table>

Renaming a File

You can easily change the name of a file using the Rename option on the File menu or by using the file's label. Remember that when you choose a filename it can contain up to 255 characters, including spaces, but it cannot contain \ ? : " < > | characters.

Practice using this feature by renaming the Sales file to give it a more descriptive filename.

To rename Sales:

1. Click the **Sales** file to select it.

2. Click the label "Sales". After a short pause a solid box outlines the label and an insertion point appears.

3. Type **Preliminary Sales Summary** as the new filename.

4. Press the **Enter key**.

5. Click the **Close** button ⊠ to close the 3 ½-inch Floppy (A:) window.

<table>
<tr><td rowspan="2">REFERENCE
window</td><td>RENAMING A FILE</td></tr>
<tr><td>■ Click the icon for the file you want to rename.
■ Click the label of the icon.
■ Type the new name for the file.
■ Press the Enter key.</td></tr>
</table>

Copying an Entire Floppy Disk

You can have trouble accessing the data on your floppy disk if the disk gets damaged, exposed to magnetic fields, or picks up a computer virus. If the damaged disk contains important files, you will have to spend many hours to try to reconstruct those files. To avoid losing all your data, it is a good idea to make a copy of your floppy disk. This copy is called a **backup** copy.

If you wanted to make a copy of an audio cassette, your cassette player would need two cassette drives. You might wonder, therefore, how your computer can make a copy of your disk if you have only one disk drive. Figure 2-21 illustrates how the computer uses only one disk drive to make a copy of a disk.

Figure 2-21 ◀
Using one disk
drive to make a
copy of a disk

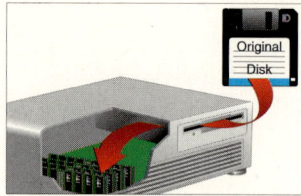

1. First, the computer copies the data from your original disk into memory.

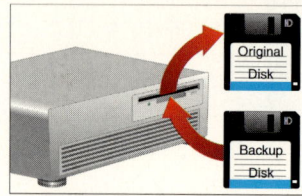

2. Once the data is in memory, you remove your original disk from the drive and replace it with your backup disk.

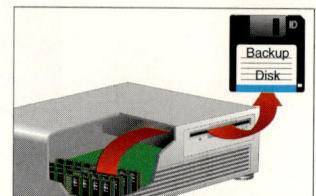

3. The computer moves the data from memory onto your backup disk.

REFERENCE window	**MAKING A BACKUP OF YOUR FLOPPY DISK**

- Click My Computer then press the Enter key.
- Insert the disk you want to copy in drive A.
- Click the 3 ½ Floppy (A:) icon [3½ Floppy (A:)] to select it.
- Click File then click Copy Disk to display the Copy Disk dialog box.
- Click Start to begin the copy process.
- When prompted, remove the disk you want to copy. Place your backup disk in drive A.
- Click OK.
- When the copy is complete, close the Copy Disk dialog box.
- Close the My Computer dialog box.

If you have two floppy disks, you can make a backup of your Student Disk now. Make sure you periodically follow the backup procedure, so your backup is up-to-date.

To back up your Student Disk:

1. Write your name and "Backup" on the label of your second disk. This will be your backup disk.

2. Make sure your Student Disk is in drive A.

3. Make sure the My Computer window is open. See Figure 2-22.

Figure 2-22 ◀
The My
Computer
window

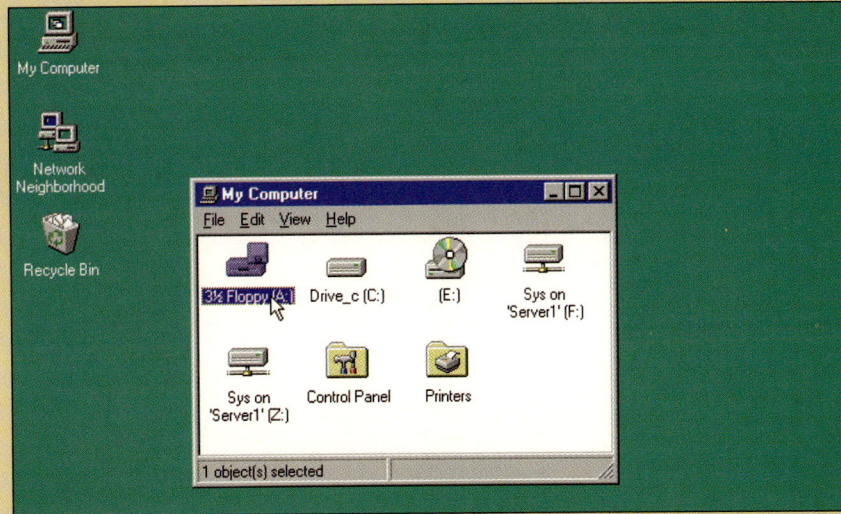

4. Click the **3 ½ Floppy (A:)** icon [icon] to select it.

   TROUBLE? If you mistakenly open the 3½ Floppy (A:) *window*, click [X].

5. Click **File**.

6. Click **Copy Disk** to display the Copy Disk dialog box as shown in Figure 2-23.

Figure 2-23 ◀
The Copy Disk
dialog box

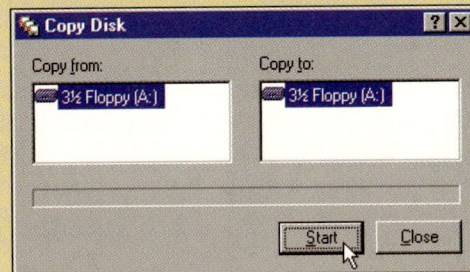

7. On the lower right side of the dialog box, you'll see a Start button. Click this **Start** button to begin the copy process.

8. When the message, "Insert the disk you want to copy from (source disk)..." appears, click the **OK** button.

9. When the message, "Insert the disk you want to copy to (destination disk)..." appears, insert your backup disk in drive A.

10. Click the **OK** button. When the copy is complete, you will see the message "Copy completed successfully."

11. After the data is copied to your backup disk, click [X] on the blue title bar of the Copy Disk dialog box.

12. Click [X] on the My Computer window to close the My Computer window.

13. Remove your disk from the drive.

Each time you make a backup, the data on your backup disk is erased, and replaced with the data from your updated Student Disk. Now that you know how to copy an entire disk, make a backup whenever you have completed a tutorial or you have spent a long time working on a file.

Quick Check

1. If you want to find out about the storage devices and printers connected to your computer, click the _____ icon.

2. If you have only one floppy disk drive on your computer, it is identified by the letter _____ .

3. The letter C: is typically used for the _____ drive of a computer.

4. What are the five pieces of information that the Details view supplies about each of your files?

5. The main directory of a disk is referred to as the _____ directory.

6. You can divide a directory into _____ .

7. If you delete the icon for a file, what happens to the file?

8. If you have one floppy disk drive, but you have two disks, can you copy a file from one floppy disk to another?

End Note

Just as you complete the Quick Check for Session 2.2, Steve appears. He asks how you are doing. You summarize what you remember from the tutorial, telling him that you learned how to insert, delete, and select text. You also learned how to work with files using Windows 95 software—you now know how to save, open, revise, and print a document. You tell him that you like the idea that these file operations are the same for almost all Windows 95 software. Steve agrees that this makes work a lot easier.

When Steve asks you if you have a supply of disks, you tell him you do, and that you just learned how to format a disk and view a list of files on your disk. Steve wants you to remember that you can use the Details view to see the filename, size, date, and time. You assure him that you remember that feature—and also how to move, delete, and rename a file.

Steve seems pleased with your progress and agrees that you're now ready to use software applications. But he can't resist giving you one last warning—don't forget to back up your files frequently!

Tutorial Assignments

1. Opening, Editing, and Printing a Document In this tutorial you learned how to create a document using WordPad. You also learned how to save, open, and print a document. Practice these skills by opening the document on your Student Disk called Resume, which is a résumé for Jamie Woods. Make the changes shown in Figure 2-24, and then print the document. After you print, save your revisions.

Figure 2-24 ◀

Change this to your name, address, and phone number. If you don't have an office number delete this.

Change this to the name of your university or college.

```
                                            JAMIE WOODS

The Envoy                                    Home (202) 328-1615
1694 Columbia Rd.  N.W.                      Office (301) 723-0345
Washington D.C.  20009

OBJECTIVE:   A challenging public relations position in the travel and tourism industry.

EDUCATION:                B.A., Journalism (to be awarded June 1996)
                          Georgetown University
                          Major:  Public Relations
                          Minor:  Psychology
                          Major G.P.A.:  3.6 / 4.0

                          Core Courses:
                          Writing for public relations
                          Magazine production and design
                          News writing and editing

PUBLIC RELATIONS
EXPERIENCE:               Public Relations Intern April - December 1994
                          Willamette Valley Visitor's Association, Eugene, OR
                          Wrote and placed news releases.
                          Served as liaison with West Coast newspapers.
                          Assisted in production of monthly newsletter.
                          Developed and managed campaign for annual
                          Willamette Valley Winery Tour.

                          Publicity Chairperson September 1993 - June 1994
                          Georgetown University Coalition for the Homeless
                          Planned successful food drive.
                          Developed public - awareness campaign.

OTHER WORK
EXPERIENCE:               Supervisor June 1994 - June 1995
                          Sherwin - Williams Company Largo, MD
                          Supervised warehouse operations and
                          eight - person staff.
                          Worked with computerized order system.

                          Inside Salesperson Summers 1993 - 1996
                          Sherwin - Williams Company Silver Spring, MD
```

2. Creating, Saving, and Printing a Letter Use WordPad to write a one-page letter to a relative or a friend. Save the document in the My Documents folder with the name "Letter." Use the Print Preview feature to look at the format of your finished letter, then print it, and be sure you sign it.

3. Managing Files and Folders Earlier in this tutorial you created a folder and moved the file called Minutes into it. Now complete a through g below to practice your file management skills.

    a. Create a folder called Spreadsheets on your Student Disk.

    b. Move the files ParkCost, Budget96, Budget97, and Sales into the Spreadsheets folder.

    c. Create a folder called Park Project.

    d. Move the files Proposal, Members, Tools, Logo, and Newlogo into the Park Project folder.

    e. Move the ParkCost file from the Spreadsheets folder to the Park Project folder.

    f. Delete the file called Travel.

    g. Switch to the Details view and answer the following questions:

Write out your answers to questions a through e.

    a. What is the largest file in the Park Project folder?

    b. What is the newest file in the Spreadsheets folder?

    c. How many files are in the root directory?

    d. How are the Members and Resume icons different?

    e. What is the file with the most recent date on the entire disk?

4. More Practice with Files and Folders For this assignment, you will format your disk again and put a fresh version of the Student Disk files on it. Complete a through h below to practice your file management skills.

    a. Format a disk.

    b. Create a Student Disk. Refer to the section "Creating Your Student Disk" in Session 2.2.

    c. Create three folders on your new Student Disk: Documents, Budgets, and Graphics.

    d. Move the files Interior, Exterior, Logo, and Newlogo to the Graphics folder.

    e. Move the files Travel, Members and Minutes to the Documents folder.

    f. Move Budget96 and Budget97 to the Budgets folder.

    g. Switch to the Details view.

Answer questions a through f.

    a. What is the largest file in the Graphics folder?

    b. How many WordPad documents are in the root directory?

    c. What is the newest file in the root directory?

    d. How many files in all folders are 5KB in size?

    e. How many files in the Documents folder are WKS files?

    f. Do all the files in the Graphics folder have the same icon?

EXPLORE

5. Finding a File Microsoft Windows 95 contains an on-line Tour that explains how to find files on a disk without looking through all the folders. Start the Windows 95 Tour (if you don't remember how, look at the instructions for Tutorial Assignment 1 in Tutorial 1), then click Finding a File, and answer the following questions:

    a. To display the Find dialog box, you must click the _____ button, then select _____ from the menu, and finally click _____ from the submenu.

    b. Do you need to type in the entire filename to find the file?

    c. When the computer has found your file, what are the steps you have to follow if you want to display the contents of the file?

6. Help with Files and Folders In Tutorial 2 you learned how to work with Windows 95 files and folders. What additional information on this topic does Windows 95 Help provide? Use the Start button to access Help. Use the Index tab to locate topics related to files and folders. Find at least two tips or procedures for working with files and folders that were not covered in the tutorial. Write out the tip in your own words and indicate the title of the Help screen that contains the information.

Lab Assignments

1. Using Files Lab In Tutorial 2 you learned how to create, save, open, and print files. The Using Files Lab will help you review what happens in the computer when you perform these file tasks. To start the Lab, follow these steps:

    a. Click the Start button.

    b. Point to Programs, then point to CTI Windows 95 Applications.

    c. Point to Windows 95 New Perspectives Brief.

    d. Click Using Files. If you can't find Windows 95 New Perspectives Brief or Using Files, ask for help from your instructor or technical support person.

Answer the Quick Check questions that appear as you work through the Lab. You can print your answers at the end of the Lab.

Using Files

Answers to Quick Check Questions

SESSION 1.1

1. a. icon b. Start button c. taskbar d. Date/Time control e. desktop f. pointer

2. Multitasking

3. Start menu

4. Lift up the mouse, move it to the right, then put it down, and slide it left until the pointer reaches the left edge of the screen.

5. Highlighting

6. If a program is running, its button is displayed on the taskbar.

7. Each program that is running uses system resources, so Windows 95 runs more efficiently when only the programs you are using are open.

8. Answer: If you do not perform the shut down procedure, you might lose data.

SESSION 1.2

1. a. title bar b. program title c. Minimize button d. Restore button e. Close button f. menu bar g. toolbar h. formatting bar i. status bar j. taskbar k. workspace l. pointer

2. a. Minimize button—hides the program so only its button is showing on the taskbar.
b. Maximize button—enlarges the program to fill the entire screen.
c. Restore button—sets the program to a pre-defined size.
d. Close button—stops the program and removes its button from the taskbar.

3. a. Ellipses—indicate a dialog box will appear.
b. Grayed out—the menu option is not currently available.
c. Submenu—indicates a submenu will appear.
d. Check mark—indicates a menu option is currently in effect.

4. Toolbar

5. a. scroll bar b. scroll box c. Cancel button d. down arrow button e. list box f. radio button g. check box

6. one, check boxes

7. On-line Help

SESSION 2.1

1. file

2. formatting

3. I-beam

4. insertion point

5. word wrap

6 You drag the I-beam pointer over the text to highlight it.

7 \ ? : * < > | "

8 extension

9 save the file again

10 paper

SESSION 2.2

1 My Computer

2 A (or A:)

3 Hard (or hard disk)

4 Filename, file type, file size, date, time

5 Root

6 Folders (or subdirectories)

7 It is deleted from the disk.

8 Yes

Windows 95 Brief Tutorials **Index**